For Tom ... For Nancy

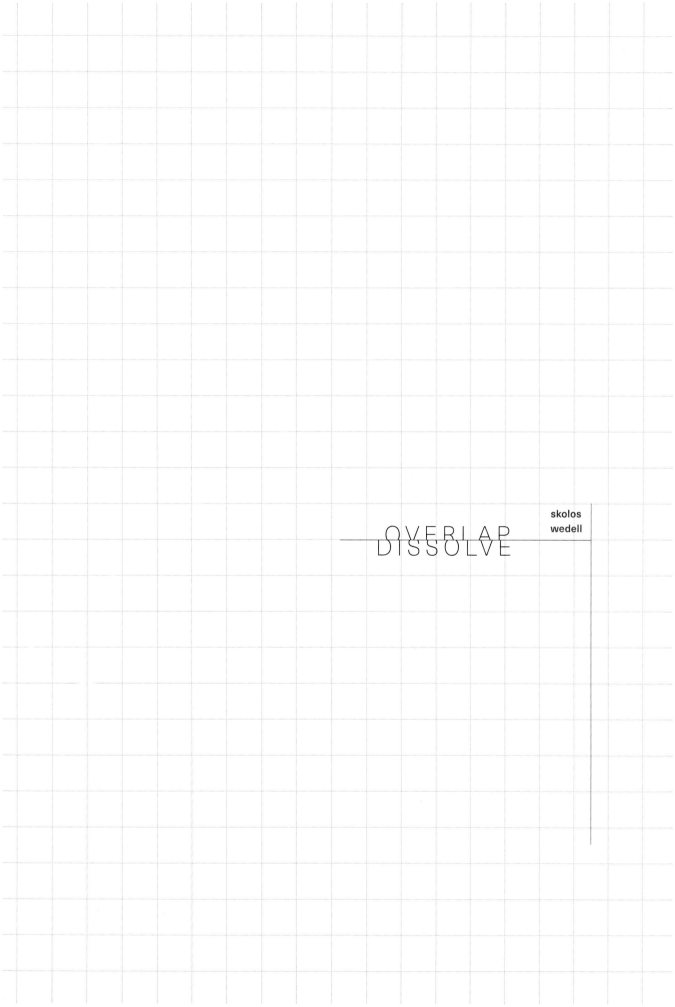

OVERLAP
DISSOLVE

skolos
wedell

OVER
DISS

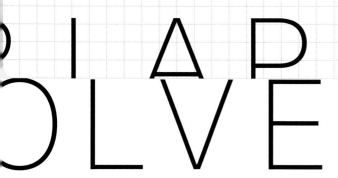

skolos
wedell

P

Preface

This book's title is adapted from that of *Overlap and Dissolve*, a retrospective of our work exhibited at Kendall College of Art and Design (KCAD) in 2019. Curator Michele Bosak came up with the title, and we think it is a perfect description of our forty-plus-year body of work and relationship. In fact, we often refer to ourselves as "two bodies and one brain."

The idea for this book emerged during our recent move from Massachusetts to Rhode Island. Packing always prompts reflection, but this time, sorting through and culling decades of printed samples and mock-ups triggered tremendous nostalgia. In the twenty years since our previous move, the content of the work and the traces of its making—paper sketches, mechanical artwork, binders of 4-by-5 inch and 8-by-10 inch Ektachrome transparencies, scale models—had become all at once strikingly archaic and fascinating. These artifacts provided a snapshot of the rapid evolution of design tools experienced by our generation, whose practices straddled the pre- and post-digital age. It felt important to examine and preserve them. That we had been there— had experienced high technology evolving—was suddenly very exciting to us.

We were reminded of how hard we had worked—more than a hundred hours per week for the first twenty years of the studio—trying to bring imagination into high-tech marketing materials. In many ways, the making of this book was motivated by remembering the youthful, industrious Tom and Nancy. We also wanted to share our experience of collaboration up close and personal. For some reason, partnership is often a mystery to graphic designers. In our case, the work itself obscures the two minds at work. In a gracious introduction to a talk I gave in Tokyo in 1996, Yusaku Kamekura said he was surprised about our work in a couple of ways: first, it looked European, not American; and second, it had such a strong, singular point of view that he was amazed when he found out it was done by two people, not one.

Collaboration sometimes raises artless questions, with people wondering: Who is really the brains behind the operation? Who really deserves the accolades for the work? What are the roles? How can they possibly be equitable? These questions, incomprehensible to us, indicate that the degree of collaboration that we have crafted is quite rare. It comes from years of experience building our sensibilities together and from a focus on the work itself, not whose idea it was. Our work encompasses a blurring of personal love and professional trust, an amalgamation of individual skills and collective discoveries.

Overlap/Dissolve exemplifies this ethos. It includes projects that fuse type and image, two- and three-dimensional space, and form and meaning to generate a multitude of combinations and transformations. Prototypes, iterations, and studio set-ups highlight the process behind the finished work, which unfolds by decade from the 1980s to the 2020s, each section beginning with a timeline of notable events. While a chronological taxonomy may seem conventional, it was critical for presenting our evolving working methods alongside emerging technologies. A pair of conversations with each other serves as the primary text, providing a direct view into our collaborative design thinking.

The book's grid subdivides the pages into two vertical and two horizontal areas with a square lower section. Enlarged poster details occupy the vertical areas to create the illusion of overlap by eclipsing images that appear in full on the neighboring spread. The design reinforces the progression of projects as one dissolves into the next and embodies the continuum of the learning process, which comprises both incremental steps forward and occasional slips backward.

We are so grateful to Andrew Blauvelt, Director of the Cranbrook Art Museum in Bloomfield Hills, Michigan, for his essay, "Reflected Realities," that contextualizes Skolos-Wedell within the history of photography and graphic design; mentor Katherine McCoy for invaluable consultation; Jennifer Liese for artful editing; and again thank Michele for our title, *Overlap/Dissolve*.

Finally, we would like to acknowledge our former partner and good friend Ken Raynor, whose dedication and hard work helped us through the studio's first decade. We are also indebted to many other collaborators within and beyond the studio's doors including assistants, clients, printers, and fabricators.

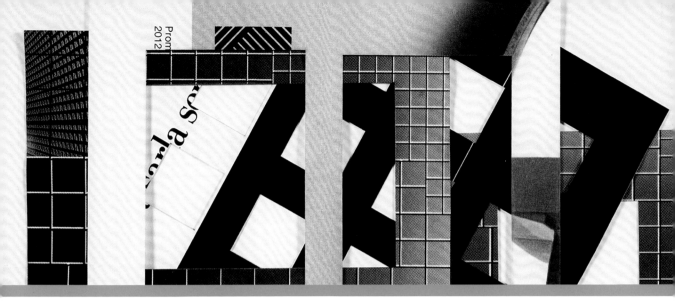

Andrew Blauvelt

Reflected

The three principals of a new design studio, circa 1980, each hold a differently shaped piece of mirrored glass in their hand, their backs to the camera. Their reflected visages stare down the viewer in what ranks among the best of such design studio portraits. In a tonal range of black, white, and grays that would make Ansel Adams proud, the portrait simultaneously conveys the seriousness and the playfulness of its creators. Carefully choreographed and lit, the image is quintessentially postmodern—contemporary yet historically, pardon the pun, reflective.

When I first saw this image in the 1980s, it brought to mind the self-portrait of the designer Herbert Bayer, who had studied and taught at the Bauhaus before emigrating to America to lend his talents to the Container Corporation of America (CCA) and the Atlantic Richfield Company (ARCO). In this now famous photograph, a 32-year-old Bayer stares at himself in the mirror, naked from the waist up. One of his arms is raised, hooked behind his head. His exposed armpit, however, has been cleanly sliced away; his other hand holds the missing piece, which is shaped like a ham hock. Bayer's facial expression communicates a blend of horror and astonishment. The image, of course, is a product of photomontage—the deliberate alteration of an image, sometimes by combining or collaging different images together or by altering or editing a photographic print or negative—a classic of surrealistic defamiliarization techniques. Bayer was among a number of European graphic designers in the first half of the twentieth century, including Piet Zwart, Paul Schuitema, Herbert Matter, Alexander Rodchenko, El Lissitzky, and Gustav Klutsis, who freely experimented with the photographic image and often combined it with bold and experimental modern typography.

Both images are just images, devoid of any verbal message or typographic elements. And this fact belies the real legacy of people like Bayer and the richness of the work of Nancy Skolos and Tom Wedell. The very definition of graphic design is the union of words and images to communicate ideas. However, despite the aforementioned pioneers, the synthesis, conflation, or integration of photographs and typography—what has been called the "typo-foto" approach of the 1920s through the 1940s—is a remarkably underexplored practice within the field. It would take Skolos and Wedell to reinvigorate the genre for contemporary graphic design decades later, beginning in the 1980s. This was not by accident, but rather by design.

Realities

The husband and wife team of Skolos and Wedell met in the 1970s as students at Cranbrook Academy of Art, a hotbed of graphic experimentation under the tutelage of another husband and wife design team, Katherine and Michael McCoy. Wedell would pursue graduate work in photography with artist-in-residence Carl Toth and design with the McCoys at Cranbrook, while Skolos would complete her undergraduate studies there as one among a small number of bachelor's degree students admitted before 1980 to the Academy, which now offers only a graduate program of study.

The merger of type and image was seeded by an era of postmodernism, which encouraged a kind of historical soul-searching that enveloped graphic design in 1970s and 1980s—in particular, an interest in avant-garde, pre-World War II modernism as an antidote to the kind of corporate modernism that had taken hold of the profession starting in the 1950s and 1960s and which had grown increasingly stale and predictable two decades on. It is not surprising therefore to see the work of Skolos and Wedell described as "techno-cubism," a portmanteau combining the high-tech design that emerged in the 1970s and 1980s, reveling in sleek, reflective, and artificial surfaces and finishes and emphasizing the constructed nature of design as an assembly of (typically) industrial pieces and Cubism, the early twentieth-century movement that featured abstract geometric forms, interpenetrating visual planes, and differing perspectives, often combined with collage techniques. Painstakingly created in the era before digital photo-editing software like Photoshop, which privileges a certain seamlessness and smoothness of photographic (un)reality, the masterfully constructed, carefully staged and photographed, and artfully collaged pre- and post-production compositions by Skolos and Wedell reveal their very constructedness and artificiality in the final iteration.

In 1976, the year Tom Wedell graduated from Cranbrook's photography program, *Artforum* published the seminal essay "The Directorial Mode: Notes Toward a Definition." In it, the critic A.D. Coleman describes a bifurcated history of photography, one dominated by the notion of image-making as an extension of a certain naturalness associated with the medium, epitomized by the idea of "capturing" the real world as it reveals itself before the camera lens. This mode, which goes essentially unnamed by Coleman, is a "responsive" form of photography, which is to say one that responds to a given subject, scene, or moment at hand. Coleman contrasts this approach with its opposite, a "directorial" mode of image-making. As the name suggests, the photographer, much like a movie director, actively arranges and constructs the images before the camera lens or further edits the results in the darkroom. Much of this minor form of photographic practice, Coleman tells us, has been dismissed by photography purists because of its use for mostly commercial purposes. It is not surprising then that the construction of the image and its integration with typography would emerge as an interest of a photographer and a designer. If the responsive, straight, or purist photographer "takes" pictures, then their directorial counterpart "makes" images—arranging, lighting, propping, editing, and constructing things for the camera. Likewise, if the conventional graphic designer merely "uses" photographs or commissions them, then their directorial counterpart "produces" images or "constructs" them.

Coleman's essay presaged the growth of an important movement of directorial mode photography in the art world of the 1980s and beyond. This movement included artists such as Cindy Sherman, who would direct herself in a series of now iconic photographs she called "film stills," and which evoked classic Hollywood movie scenes; Nic Nicosia and Jeff Wall, whose images restaged historical paintings or cinematic-like events; Victor Shrager, who arranged still lifes of printed ephemera collaged before the camera lens; Barbara Kasten, who created colorfully lit tableaux of abstract shapes; and Sandy Skoglund, whose surrealistic scenes of sculpted figures are deployed in multiples across phantasmagoric scenes.

In rare instances in the world of graphic design, constructed images and typographic compositions also emerged in the 1970s and 1980s. For example, the work of photographer Jayme Odgers and graphic designer April Greiman used so-called "deep space photography," which featured dramatic scale changes to figures and objects in a scene along with fore-shortening and cast shadows to further heighten pictorial depth. The typography would often, however, remain a distinct, if sympathetic, graphic layer of its own. About a decade after Skolos and Wedell left Cranbrook, the department and its alumni would find itself exploring the use of staged photography through my own work as well as that of Allen Hori, Scott Zukowski, Jane Kosstrin and David Sterling, Richelle Huff, P. Scott Makela, and Robert Nakata, among others. Nakata working at Studio Dumbar on a series of posters for the Holland Festival with photographer Lex van Pieterson in the late 1980s would perhaps come closest to reflecting Skolos and Wedell's typographic and photographic integration.

It is, however, the dedicated use and evolution of the practice of staged photography and integrated typography for more than four decades that stands Skolos and Wedell apart from their contemporary peers and historical predecessors. So much has changed within the practice of graphic design and photography since they began working in this way, including the introduction of digitally aided design tools that have transformed both typography and photography, rendering those analog practices nearly anachronistic. Paradoxically, the tableaux created by Skolos and Wedell, whether in front of camera or recomposed in the computer, today seem to be wholly digitally conceived and produced. When they began using this process in the 1980s, computer graphics were still striving for the kinds of complicated reflections, simulated lighting, and complex layering of objects in their software that photographers, designers, and artists had previously achieved on their own. Such software successfully simulates reality in the computer for the average designer today. The staged compositions of Skolos and Wedell, by contrast, take on an almost nostalgic quality, wherein the sense of craft and the charm of the assembled scene speaks to a humanness of care, attention to detail, and creative inventiveness that far exceeds the virtual.

That original portrait of Tom Wedell, Nancy Skolos, and former partner Kenneth Raynor ironically captures the very people who are somehow missing in the many posters created by Skolos and Wedell. Their spaces and scenes are, in fact, absent of any human subject—an intentional, early blind spot acknowledged by Wedell. It is only when a camera, another camera, intrudes upon the scene that they are caught in the act of constructing their imagined worlds. A photograph documenting the designers at work on a 1991 poster for the furniture expo NeoCon could serve as a bookend to the 1980 studio portrait. In it, the two carefully attend to the details of their constructed reality—a can of compressed air and a Staticmaster brush to remove specks of dust in hand—the man and woman behind the lens tidying up the scene while pulling all the proverbial levers.

1969 Tom receives Certificate in Photography, Layton School of Art, Milwaukee

1973 Tom receives BFA University of Michigan, School of Architecture and Design

1973 Nancy studies Industrial Design at the University of Cincinnati

1975 Tom and Nancy meet at Cranbrook Academy of Art

1976 Tom receives MFA Cranbrook Academy of Art, Department of Photography

1977 Tom studies design, Cranbrook Academy of Art, Department of Design

1977 Nancy receives BFA Cranbrook Academy of Art, Department of Design

1977–1979 Tom takes first teaching job as Instructor at the Swain School of Design, Department of Graphic Design, New Bedford, MA

1979 Nancy receives MFA Yale University, School of Art, Department of Graphic Design

1979 Nancy and Tom are married at Cranbrook Academy of Art

1979 Skolos, Wedell + Raynor is founded, Boston, MA

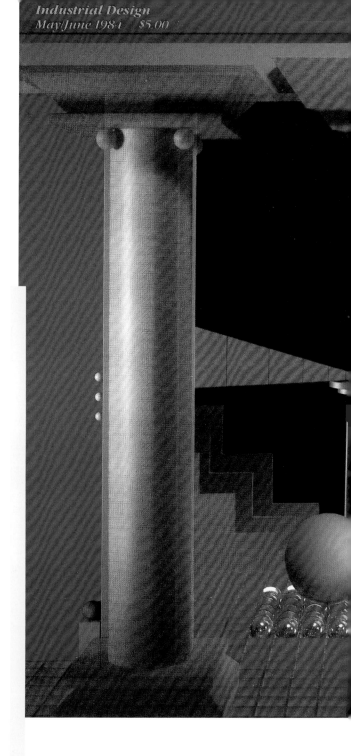

Industrial Design
May/June 1984 $5.00

Overlap/Dissolve:
An Introduction in
Five Parts

M
T

Modernism and Technology

Fernand Léger, *Mechanical Elements*, 1918–23, oil on canvas, 83 ⅛ × 66 in., Kunstmuseum, Basel

Our studio was born in Boston in 1979 in conjunction with the rise of high technology and accompanied by an urgent demand for its visual representation and marketing. The specialized electronics and computer-related subject material we were being asked to interpret became more and more abstract as the technology advanced from electronic components like speaker drivers, video projectors, and high-speed printers to elaborate computer circuitry and software. It was a dramatically transitional time.

Our clients were often passionate geniuses with tremendous drive. We spent whole afternoons watching them demonstrate their products, patiently drawing diagrams so we could understand their innovations. Even though our capacity for science, like their aptitude for art, was superficial at best, they opened our imagination and drove us to visually depict these radical technologies.

We didn't realize it at the time, but the work we were making was a visceral response to the content as it was being processed through the lenses of two young designers educated in late-modernist art schools. Contemporary art and design education is finally moving away from Bauhaus-focused teaching, opening, thankfully, to broader influences. As students in the late 1970s, however, we were indoctrinated with modernist principles. For us, the patterns, forms, and speed of technology recalled purist geometric shapes and futurist motion; engineering concepts, explained through diagrams, had an elemental energy that tapped into constructivism; the complexity of technology echoed both the simultaneity of cubism and the impossibility of surrealism.

Max Ernst, *Two Children are Threatened by a Nightingale*, 1924, oil with painted wood and printed paper elements, 27 ½ × 22 ½ × 4 ½ in., Museum of Modern Art, New York

El Lissitzky, *Beat the Whites with the Red Wedge*, 1920, color lithograph, printed in red and black on off-white wove paper, 20 1/16 × 24 7/16 in., Museum of Fine Arts, Boston

We will never forget the first time we heard the word *software* and were told to think of it as the opposite of hardware. "Like pillows and blankets?" we asked. It was 1983 and the software package being explained, Digital Equipment's ALL-IN-1, synchronized multiple office tasks and could be reconfigured and expanded. "It's so beautiful," the client pronounced, "it's like a chambered nautilus

Reynolds-DeWalt
Printing Poster
(in process,
illustrating color
offset printing), 1981

ID magazine, May/June
1984, cover design and
photography

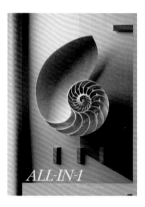

Digital Equipment
Corporation,
ALL-IN-1 Poster, 1983,
offset lithograph,
32 × 26 in.

Kloss Video
Corporation,
Videobeam Poster,
1985, offset
lithograph,
36 × 36 in.

shell that grows with you." This metaphor led to the staging of a surrealist-inspired poster that situated a nautilus shell, painted flat white, within a beach-colored geometric surround, not unlike an office cubicle. To express the inner workings of the software, we superimposed a diagram onto the shell's edges using the newly developed Scitex digital retouching system. This marked the beginning of the computer becoming part of our creative process.

Back then, however, the predominance of saturated color and geometric forms in our work often made it appear computer-generated even when it wasn't. In 1984, an engineer from Caltech, having seen a cover we designed for *ID* magazine, called the studio and insisted we had developed a computer-aided design program to create the cover's image. It took quite a while to convince him that it was simply a studio photograph, with painted geometric elements, set up on an under-lit plastic ceiling grid. To us, this handmade process was second nature. At that time, we still did things the way they were done before computer-aided photo assembly and retouching capabilities came along, when specialists carefully cut, inlaid, and dyed large format transparencies; when illusions of layering and motion were attained with multiple exposures, sometimes moving film holders between two large-format view camera set-ups. We knew what it was like to conduct test runs in the lab and spend hours waiting for results.

By the early 1990s we had thoroughly welcomed the transition to digital photography and desktop photo composition. The ability to immediately see the images, enlarge them, correct misalignments, identify flaws in the set-up, adjust exposure, and make multiple versions without prohibitive film processing costs greatly accelerated the creative process. The digital environment also allowed us to see the images in context, in design layout programs, and to produce variations that could quickly be shared with collaborators. As technology advanced, we did too, moving from the analog to the digital, riding the learning curve, and pushing our craft forward.

2+3
D

Two and Three Dimensions

The three-dimensional aspect of our work was largely informed by our interdisciplinary education at Cranbrook, where we met in 1975. While both of us had previous three-dimensional training, it was our mentors Katherine and Michael McCoy who presented design as a unified endeavor encompassing product, print, interior design, and furniture. Cranbrook as a whole embodied design not as a singular discipline but as a way of life.

This early exposure to crossing disciplines and entering less-studied territory stimulated an uninhibited sense of experimentation that we brought to our graphic design work, sometimes directly. For example, the form and materials of the "Crystal Chair," which we designed as an entry for *Progressive Architecture* magazine's 1983 Conceptual Furniture Competition, inspired the second Berkeley Typographers Poster (p. 51) that came soon after it. (The chair, which was missing a front leg so it couldn't be sat upon, won an award.)

In the postmodernist 1980s, we scoured the Italian architecture magazines *Domus* and *Abitare*, and as architects became our clients, architecture took hold in our design thinking. The Lyceum Fellowship's annual competition for architecture students has been a focus for us ever since its founding in 1986. Each year the competition's program is developed by a preeminent architect; our charge is to develop the poster and ancillary materials, conveying the character of the assignment without suggesting a specific solution.

We construct the posters' images first as three-dimensional models, their forms and surfaces shaped by characteristics of the proposed site, required structures, and functions. The success of the photographic image hinges on both the symbolic (design) and the physical (constructed) qualities of the model. Lighting amplifies its structural and textural qualities. The translation of these

Opposite: Digital Equipment Corporation Capabilities Brochure (in process, three-dimensional model and lighting set-up), 1992

Crystal Chair, 1983, Plexiglass and sheet metal, scale model: 1 in. = 1 ft. (*Progressive Architecture* magazine Conceptual Furniture Design Competition Award)

Skolos-Wedell Home and Studio, 1999, Canton, Massachusetts, Jon McKee and Mark Hutker and Associates, Architects

Skolos, Wedell + Raynor Studio, Charlestown, Massachusetts (floorplan and photo studio), 1985

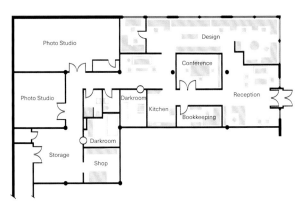

three-dimensional forms through photography into two-dimensional posters is the most critical moment in our process. The images must maintain their intrinsic structural integrity while also being open enough to accept additional typography and graphic elements. A balance of image and text achieves the holistic message.

Alongside our graphic design and photography practice, we have also designed interior spaces, starting with our own studio space in 1985. Like many new designers, we began our studio in our apartment and gradually expanded—first into the basement and a second floor, and finally into a 5,000-square-foot commercial studio space that included two photo studios, two darkrooms, a conference room, a kitchen, and a large design area. Clients who visited enjoyed the space and its furnishings and commissioned us to design their homes and office interiors. Our projects often included designing custom furniture and carpets, providing us with ever-expanding opportunities to discover new forms and materials. Designing interior spaces not only honed our awareness of contemporary furnishings and fixtures, textiles and color palettes, it also came full circle, contributing to the intricacy and material qualities of our small-scale photographic models.

In 1999 we integrated our life and work into a home/studio, located halfway between Boston and Providence and designed by Lyceum Fellowship clients Jon McKee and Mark Hutker. We collaborated with them to select the materials—copper and silver ribbed aluminum and a translucent fiberglass wall system—creating an interior space that some have compared to a life-size version of one of our photographic models. After almost twenty years there, in 2017 we moved to Providence, where our current home/studio is the former residence of architect Ira Rakatansky and family. His compact modernist design provides ambient inspiration, and we enjoy an even more seamless lifestyle for teaching, working, and living.

P
M
Processes and Materials

Berkeley Typographers
Poster (in process, set-up for
photo shoot with Plexiglas,
perforated metal, and styrene
model), 1989

Perhaps the most distinctive quality in our graphic design work is the way in which it incorporates photography of materials and constructed objects that simultaneously represent symbols and evoke sensation through light and shadow. From the beginning, we planned every project in phases, including drawing, constructing miniature test models, and choosing the materials for the fabrication of the final three-dimensional design. This process was a natural extension of the analog skills we had developed to generate mechanical artwork for printing. Making mechanicals involved carefully cutting type from paper galleys with an X-ACTO knife and adhering the pieces of type along with FPO ("for position only") black-and-white photostats to illustration board at full scale. We placed instructions for the printer on layers of acetate to indicate the size and position of images and on a tracing paper overlay hand-colored with pencils or markers to indicate ink colors.

Our research into a wide variety of materials and testing them in the photo studio represents both art and science. We recorded colored papers, fabrics, reflective materials, perforated metals, and textured papers on film, experimenting with lighting and color and cataloging them for future application. Each surface was further tested for flexibility, rigidity, and molding properties to determine its use value for structures and sets. Some

Flat file of colored paper
scraps used to create
compositional grids, 1990

materials fell flat in front of the camera and others came to life in unexpected ways—especially when applied to three-dimensional shapes that caught the light to create remarkable effects. Over time, our models became more intentional, engineered with openings and angles to create optimal textures, highlights, and shadows.

Delphax Fonts Poster (in process, textured rubber sheets and Plexiglas jigsaw-cut letters spray painted in metallic colors), 1987

Lyceum Fellowship Poster (in process, fabricating balloon-molded rocks to create a desert scene), 2011

It wasn't that the materials themselves necessarily sparked the solution for a particular project, but their structural and symbolic characteristics always entered the creative process. Sometimes the subject of the project suggested a material, as in the Reynolds-DeWalt Printing poster (p. 47), where the notion of cones shaped from mylar sheets came directly from looking at the cylinders in an offset printing press. Another example, the Berkeley Typographers poster (p. 51), was made of black-and-white dotted fabric to suggest the high-contrast quality of typography. For the Delphax Fonts poster (p. 75) we arrived at a collection of metallic surfaces made by spray-painting textured rubber panels to recall the tactility of metal type.

An unforeseen benefit arose while assembling the models. Discarded paper scraps at the edges of our worktables caught our eye and captured our imagination. We often saved them and arranged them into potential grid structures for future projects. Because this strategy proved prolific, we began to cultivate chance operations by making collages from cut-up magazines. The fluid to-and-fro between form and content and image and symbol in the collages was more intuitive than theoretical, a serendipitous methodology that accelerated our experimental model construction process. The Lyceum 2011 poster (p. 187), for example, based on a program situated in the Great Salt Desert, suggested organic, geological imagery and sparked us to use balloon-formed plaster to create exaggerated "rock" formations. Our cumulative knowledge about images, structures, and material properties set the stage for openness in and interconnection between every phase of our process.

C
C
Collage and Composition

Collage can provide endless inspiration for graphic designers and is a fruitful starting point for many of our projects. Everything in a designer's vocabulary—words, ephemera, materials, and colors—can be recombined to create unique visual and verbal phenomena. Unexpected formal arrangements engage both our minds and eyes and challenge our preconceptions.

Our interest in collage and the way it encouraged us to let go of a deliberate process originated in the early stages of our careers, while working with "paste ups." In creating these pre-press mechanicals, we quickly realized that scraps at the edge of the drawing board and leftover cut-up paper provided more visual interest than the projects we were intentionally "designing." Mining paper scraps from our studio storage drawers, we began to create asymmetric compositions that could be translated into "grids." The grids could later be used to assist in type placement or re-imagined as three-dimensional structures for photography.

In the late 1990s and early 2000s we moved beyond simple colored paper scraps and began to experiment with cut-up pieces of magazines. The abundance and variety of both image and type elements within each magazine piece resulted in compositions with multiple vanishing points, scale shifts, and font variations. The

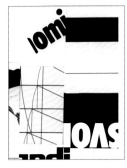

random mixing of these decontextualized yet content-rich visual elements activated dynamic formal arrangements and provocative symbolic associations, opening possibilities for extraordinary visual/verbal phenomena.

We made batches of collages, usually on weekends, with no specific project in mind. Then, at the start of a new design assignment, we reviewed our backlog to see if there were any that might fit the subject at hand. Surveying the collage archive required extreme focus, as we examined each one to envision how its structure and content might work to energize the project's subject and format. Once we selected a handful of candidates, we would sketch them on tracing paper,

modifying the forms and imagining essential words that fit the shape of the type fragments, while also preserving the distinct formal relationships that heightened the meaning of our topic. Examples showing the sequence of steps from collage to finished projects are included throughout these pages.

Many historical precedents also influenced us. The collage technique was introduced to modern art in the early twentieth century by Georges Braque and Pablo Picasso, who began with cutting and pasting painted surfaces and quickly applied real-world materials (for example, chair caning) directly onto the canvas. This milestone in the development of Western art sparked questions about what constitutes a work of art and inspired generations of artists that followed. Looking at Braque and Picasso as well as Hannah Höch, Kurt Schwitters, Man Ray, László Moholy-Nagy, and others expanded our thinking about how collage might be applied to graphic design. Höch's work used collage to expose the chaos of modern life through a buildup of energetic pictorial elements and unexpected convergences. Schwitters believed that the act of collage released intrinsic magical qualities in the constituent pieces that only came alive in juxtaposition. Moholy-Nagy took a more diagrammatic approach, illustrating human conditions such as *Jealousy* (1927) with

designed photographic assemblies. We were also interested in the machine-made qualities of early twentieth-century collage, which reinforced the link between the tools that made them and their industrial era. We kept this context in mind as we worked with collage in the digital realm.

In teaching, we have employed collage techniques to make intuition more tangible for students. Our chopped-up magazine scraps become the catalyst for an exercise in how content and form can be more seamlessly negotiated. Stirring up thousands of scrap pieces with the resulting "happy accidents" of unexpected shape, scale, and color automatically sparks the give-and-take of a fluid creative process and quickly broadens students' experience with type, image, and composition.

Type and Image

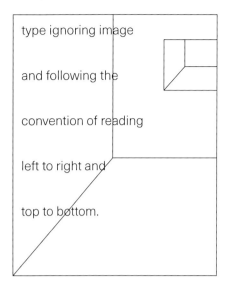

type ignoring image

and following the

convention of reading

left to right and

top to bottom.

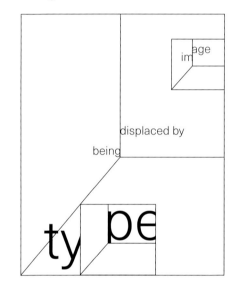

3. Fragmentation

image

displaced by

being

type

It has often been said that a picture is worth a thousand words. More recently, in a lecture at the Rhode Island School of Design, multimedia designer Mikon van Gastel offered, "One perfectly chosen word is worth thirty minutes of footage." Value judgments aside, one thing is clear: graphic designers are both blessed and cursed for working with two very distinct modes of communication: the word and the image.

As in any successful partnership, type and image work best when they complement each other—when they finish each other's sentences. For graphic designers, a photograph isn't finished with a click of the shutter. That is just the beginning of the creative process, as image becomes a part of a piece of graphic design. In fact, the image must be "incomplete" so there is something left for the type to do.

In the conceptual phase of a project, designers often begin working with type and image intuitively, in a mind space where the two are more like substances rather than entities. We experience them, imagine them, see them in our sleep, and consider them simultaneously. They never operate outside of a context, and their meaning is never fully realized until they are put into play. Often they are assigned a "format" within which to interact. They can be visualized with common textures, shapes, and colors, and unified with light or shadow, but even in the realm of our greatest imagination, remain uniquely discernible as type or image.

The viewer depends on type and image to give form and meaning to many messages and ideas. Both contain room for interpretation by the viewer and extend the role of the graphic designer from form giver to mediator and guide. Through form, designers construct and create an organized system for content, emphasizing some concepts and de-emphasizing others, providing ways into, around, and out of each work.

Reprinted Introduction from *Type, Image, Message* (Rockport, 2006)

2. Fusion

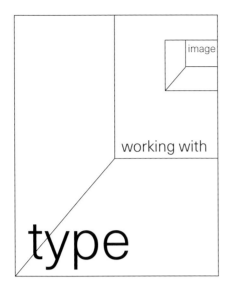

4. Inversion

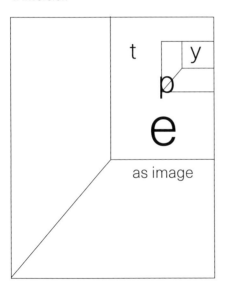

Diagrams from the book show four critical relationships between typographic space and photographic space.

While illustrated here as stand-alone scenarios, more than one of these conditions may exist in any given piece.

While much has been written on typography and photography, surprisingly little has been written about how the two work together. Many times, while in the final throes of completing a project that employs both type and image, designers will confess, "I'm just no good with type." The reality is that nobody is naturally good at combining type and image. Even though words and images are familiar ways of expressing human experience, the two forms of communication are inherently difficult to reconcile.

Space and Point(s) of Entry

"Reading" a photograph is very different from reading a text. For example, in Western culture, a conventional hierarchy is well established, dictating a left to right, top to bottom approach. Letters make up words, words make up sentences, and sentences make up concepts. It is a primarily linear construction that cannot be easily rearranged without affecting meaning.

Photographs are representations of the physical world possessing a three-dimensional sense of time and space. For example, photographs of landscapes feature a horizon, while photographs of architecture contain perspective and a vanishing point. Portraits contain unique human features of eyes, nose, and mouth. Each of these elements and scenarios commands a different point of entry into a picture.

Unlike objects rendered in photographic space, letters and their forms do not customarily exist in three-dimensional space. Letterforms themselves have no intrinsic third dimension. Jan Tschichold, renowned typographer and book designer, wrote a wonderful metaphorical essay about working with type called "Clay in the Potter's Hand." But type is less like clay and more like Legos. It is a prefabricated kit of parts, a closed system, with typefaces that contain inner harmonies that make them complete in and of themselves.

Contrast, Color, Texture

While images render the world in a complete tonal range, tonal shifts generally interfere with, more than contribute to, the clear reading of text. Type is therefore an inherently high-contrast medium. Dieter Feseke of the Berlin-based studio Umbra-Dor observes, "The type is more geometry, more digital and clean. The image is patchy, spotted, more analog, natural, and dirty."

As one views and discovers a work that is formed of both entities, the flow of experience is varied, with each medium dictating its own point of entry and rate of comprehension. The reading gets even more intricate when the piece contains multiple images and text elements. Complexity adds to the time needed to investigate and interpret a work, regulated by each viewer's level of experience. For intricacy to transcend entanglement, designers must embrace the creative potential of photo-typographic space. These strategies should guide the viewer beyond what Rick Poyner, in his book *No More Rules: Graphic Design and Postmodernism*, calls "fully postmodern representational space, where all that is solid often melts into an intoxicating, semi-abstract blur."

Meaning

As containers for meaning and expressions of human experience, type and image have different properties—but they also operate on different levels of cognition.

It is important to note that "type" in the context of this discussion refers to the phonetic alphabet. In *Understanding Media*, Marshall McLuhan noted that unlike the Chinese ideogram that retains inclusive associations, "As an intensification and extension of the visual function, the phonetic alphabet diminishes the role of the other senses of sound and touch and taste ... " And later on, when discussing the photograph, he observed: "If the phonetic alphabet was a technical means of severing the spoken word from aspects of sound and gesture, the photograph and its development in the movie restored gesture to the human technology of recording experience."

Images open the door to multiple interpretations through varied levels of experience, memory, and their associations. These connections make photography a more complex, and more visceral form of communication. Words, contrary to images, are essentially shapes that have learned, recognized meanings. Willi Kunz describes this phenomenon in *Typography: Macro- and Microaesthetics:* "Every word is comprised of a particular set of letters, whose sequence and form makes each word semantically and syntactically unique."

Lyceum Fellowship Poster, 2006, employs multiple type and image relationships.

Fusion

The Lyceum logo, representing the constancy of the annual competition is fused to the perspective of the image.

Separation

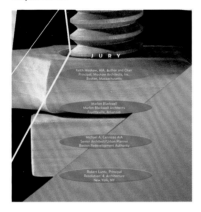

Information specific to the 2006 competition, its jury, and title, float on mediating graphic elements (ellipses and zigzags) over the image.

Fragmentation

The date, "2006," is fragmented to express the vitality and animation of a new competition program.

Words are forms that only communicate to those who understand the specific code of that language. Words, while potentially harboring some ambiguities based on exposure and additional learned references, are a more explicit form of communication.

When type meets image there is automatically a dialogue between them and each can pull the other in many different directions. The multi-indexical nature of the photographic image is paired with the more concise content of the text. The text can support or contradict the image just as the image can illustrate or refute the written message. Each may also contain independent meanings that may react with or against the message in the work. To compound the interpretation further, additional relationships can spring up from the viewer's background and personal associations. In his essay "The Photographic Message," Roland Barthes said of the interaction of text and image: "It is true that there is never a real incorporation since the substances of the two structures (graphic and iconic) are irreducible, but there are most likely degrees of amalgamation."

Four Critical Relationships

During the process of analyzing the photo-typographic works contained in these pages, the difficulty of teasing out the visual from the verbal brought the struggle between the two forms of communication to the forefront, but four noticeable categories of interaction began to emerge.

1. Separation: when the type and image operate independently, and both the text and image retain a clear level of autonomy. Separation allows the text to react with, against, or independently from the image using frames, compartments, or layers.

2. Fusion: when the type and image merge into one entity through a unifying force such as optics, surface, or perspective that synthesizes the type, the image, and meaning to present a strong visual coherence—a "cause and effect" that is immediately apparent to the viewer

3. Fragmentation: when the type and image disturb or disrupt one another, usually with one or the other being the aggressor, suggesting a state of flux. Unlike fusion where motion is a unifying element, in fragmentation, the elements are not evenly acted upon. While the force of fusion is to homogenize, the action of fragmentation is more uneven and unpredictable, not unlike a weather pattern.

4. Inversion: a specific form of fusion where the type and image trade places and the type takes on pictorial properties or the image takes on typographic qualities.

In Conversation: No Obstacles, Only Possibilities

N   How about we start by talking about one of the things people ask about most: our collaborative practice. Because our work has a strong point of view, people are often surprised that it is made collaboratively.

T   Yes, it's like a tennis game—one person serves to the other and the other sends it back, and you realize you're playing the game and the ideas go back and forth and eventually connect and synchronize.

N   How did you know you could trust me as a collaborator?

T   Because you're a strong designer and you're smart. I could tell that immediately. You're not egocentric, you're really interested, the same way I'm interested, in the work itself. You ask the important questions: How is this piece going to look? What will it take to get it there? Am I going to get the best result to communicate the message?

N   Our pieces are not necessarily even, 50/50 collaborations, and it's not like one person always does the same parts of the process. How would you outline the phases of our process and our roles?

T   It's always difficult to tell what comes first—the chicken or the egg idea. Who takes the lead and who lends the support? But someone usually has a main idea. For example, you started the process for the Delphax Fonts poster (p. 75) with a complete drawing of a kind of cubist-looking assembly of parts. We both had an interest in incorporating textures and surfaces from our library of materials and we began constructing a model that followed your initial idea. It turned out a little different from the drawing, but it was still the same design, reinterpreted by the way the materials went together and the camera work. That would be an early example of something 75 to 80 percent yours.

Then later on—off the top of my head—I remember getting excited by of the use of optics to magnify letterforms for the Honoring Matthew Carter poster (p. 182). You typeset the letters and I moved them around to create the composition for the photograph while thinking about how type can be magnified. That's another example that's almost the opposite of the Fonts poster, probably 80 percent mine in a way, but it was still collaborative because in every phase of our work

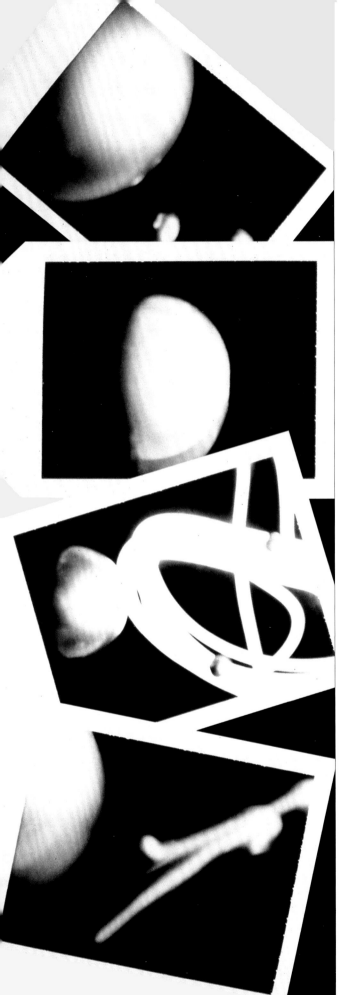

we always ask the other person, "What do you think of that?" It's like always having a consultant there and mentoring each other and challenging each other to move forward. The initial idea and the execution get blended, even more so now.

N After I completed the first Berkeley Typographers poster (p. 48), which was basically just graphic, you suggested that the second (p. 51) should be photographic and you were insistent. I think that was a real turning point. For materials, we went to the fabric store with no real idea of what we were going to do. Intuitively, as I remember, we picked out polka dot fabrics—mostly black and white with a variety of opacities and dot sizes. It was kind of like that movie …

T *Close Encounters of the Third Kind* (1977), where Richard Dreyfuss starts building mountains out of dirt piles. We weren't really sure why we were drawn to the cloth, but the dots were very graphic, and we were excited to see how the collection of transparent, dotted fabric, in combination with in-camera modifications such as multiple exposures and various lighting techniques, could create something surprising. The dots made an appearance again in the third Berkeley Typographers poster (p. 52) as perforated metal, but the central idea for that poster was the typesetter's new capability of setting type in place on the page.

N You can retrofit meaning into the black-and-white dots as related to typography, but it wasn't a conscious intention or association at the time. We got a little more directed toward meaning in the work toward the late '80s and early '90s.

Honoring Matthew
Carter Poster
(detail), 2010

Opposite: Berkeley
Typographers Poster
(detail), 1989

T   Yes, much more directed, and less
     abstract. After we had been teaching for
     some time and dealing with semiotics
     as we were at school, our brains were
     triggered back into earlier interests—
     symbols, meaning, and their use in
     representing ideas. Placing them into
     the work became very exciting and
     generative.

     The miniature sets we designed for the
     Lyceum posters, for example, made
     space for shaping meaning in architec-
     ture. The Lyceum competition audience
     is focused and knowledgeable, consisting
     of students and teachers in architec-
     ture. The jury chair is always someone
     who works on the leading edge of archi-
     tectural ideas and provides a program
     that allows a lot of room for interpre-
     tation. We can pull key concepts from
     each program to represent in the poster,
     promoting the competition without
     attempting to solve the competition
     problem. Constructing meaning though
     model-making is always very much at
     play in the Lyceum posters. We almost
     become architects of ideas through
     designing our structures.

N   Would you say that you approach pho-
     tography differently as a graphic designer
     rather than a photographer?

T   Herbert Matter looked at photography
     as a method of graphic representation.
     But when he photographed a product for
     Knoll, for example, the cues were always
     taken from the product. In "designed"
     photography, like what we do, we're
     using words and images derived from
     concepts and ideas, and that's a different
     kind of process—a much more flexible
     process because it's not restricted by
     any "real" object that dictates having to
     be represented in a clear, concise

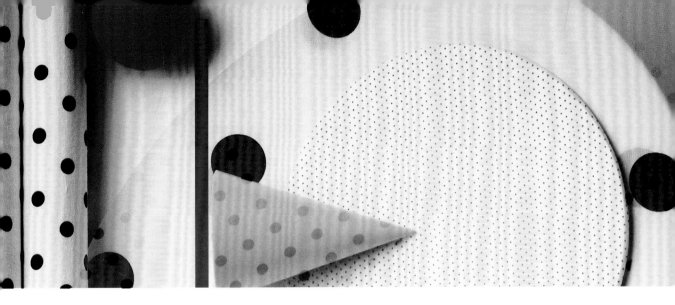

fashion. The trick is to develop a kind of organic, open-ended thinking as a way of working with the photographic image. It takes years really, but I have gradually become more fluid with image-making and designing pictures where symbols and forms naturally coalesce.

N   Your distinction makes me think about the difference between drawing from life versus drawing from imagination. When you design your photographs and craft them using materials, space, and light, how does the image begin to take shape and move from your mind to your hand to your eye?

T   The image comes from so many different places. It comes from our discussions of course, or sometimes it's inspired by a visual form, like the collages, or an object, like the lenses in the Honoring Matthew Carter poster (p. 182), or just simple words. Somebody says something or you read something in the brief and it creates an image in your mind's eye. It seems like we mix all of those inspirations together now. Before, it came from one source, but now a collection of sources feeds the process.

N   What's your favorite part of the creative process?

T   The most challenging, exciting, and terrifying moment is the beginning. When you are given an assignment and you get an inspiration, you know you're going to end up with something—you have to have something at the end—but the path to getting there is not predetermined. You have to wander around for a while. I think Mike McCoy said it best when I was working on photographing one of his products. He described me as a shark swimming around for the longest time before I'd go in to "attack." With more experience and with the two of us working together I don't "swim around" very long anymore. You'll say something, I'll say something, we'll think about it, and we'll both go after the whole thing.

N   I get more nervous once we have an idea because it's challenging to keep it alive and not overwork it. Sometimes we embellish things too much. It's hard to have perspective.

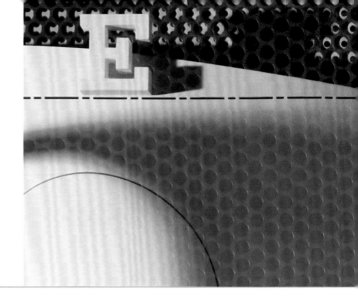

Berkeley Typographers
Poster (detail), 1986

Opposite: Berkeley
Typographers Poster
(detail), 1989

Looking back on our archive, knowing that we're both really self-critical, what strengths and weaknesses do you see?

T   Overworking, as you said, is a weakness, or missing the boat or misinterpreting objectives or getting distracted and going off in the wrong direction.

      I think four things make great artists or designers: curiosity, focus, grit, and acute judgment. Judgment—the ability to call yourself on things and say, "You know, this isn't right, that should be better!"—is so important. Sometimes we don't quite get to that fourth item, sometimes because we're too focused. What moves a good or mediocre piece to greatness is having those four things working in harmony.

N   How do you think teaching has influenced our process?

T   It has really keyed me in to a better way of thinking. When you teach, you have to be able to maintain a lightness and an intellectual agility. That's the best part about it—you really have to think about the ramifications of what you're going to say, how it's going to affect people, possible interpretations, and what students will do with the project. You have to think of five solutions for every one that a student might come up with, so your mind is being trained to be flexible. I think that helps the process, our process.

N   So much of this book is devoted to posters. Poster design plays a marginal role in visual communication practice these days, especially in the U.S. so we've been surprisingly fortunate to design so many over the years. I think of poster design as it exists today as a sport, with international poster biennials and triennials operating like a graphic design Olympics. We've met so many incredible designers through those networks and we all share a passion for posters.

      What do you think attracts you to the poster as a form?

T   First, scale and how things can be expressed at a scale.

N   What does scale afford?

T   It affords, for someone with a quiet voice, a bigger voice. Impact. It gives the designer plenty of playing field on which to execute both subtle and "loud" modes of expression. The range is greater. It's like writing a symphony versus a little tune you sing in the shower. There's a unique magnitude you achieve in a poster-size image.

I love narrative and film, but I am also drawn to the fixed image. Freezing time grants viewers the ability to hold that moment and concentrate and absorb a lot of details. Photographs do that, and posters really do that. There's a moment of contemplation that motion pieces don't have. I watch a lot of films many times and still feel the loss of detail due to the limited time spent with each scene.

N   I think by using photography we were able to take cubist concepts of simultaneity in new directions by using the camera to capture multiple points of view and then assemble different points of view into one image. Those visual concepts are even more magical to see in photographs.

T   Our early experiments with multiple exposures for the Boston Acoustics poster (p. 43) were formative in this way. We wanted to evoke a sense of sound and vibration but we had a product—a speaker, basically a box—that was not so inspiring. Our concept was to create the gesture of sound with a combination of multiple exposures using a 4 × 5 view camera and to make it look like this thing was moving. It was a very simple technique that now would be done in a computer, but then you had to do it in the camera.

N   I was really astounded by the Boston Acoustics photo shoot because you knew what you were doing but I didn't. I kept wondering, "Is this going to work?"

T   Yes, that was an experiment in terror. It is also an example of a project where our idea gained momentum, it didn't stagnate, and we didn't kill it. Which moments do you remember as being critical?

N   Starting to work with you on the Yale Symphony Orchestra posters and seeing the potential of images as graphic design was the first big moment for me. I was familiar with the beautiful, dramatic image/text posters in the Swiss design canon, but it was exciting to think about putting our heads together to "design with photography" in a different way.

Even with the first Yale Symphony Orchestra poster, the Organizational Meeting announcement (p. 36), I remember how we put letterforms on vibrating wires and watching you expose the image directly onto Kodalith high-contrast film at full size, so we could print it directly as a blueprint.

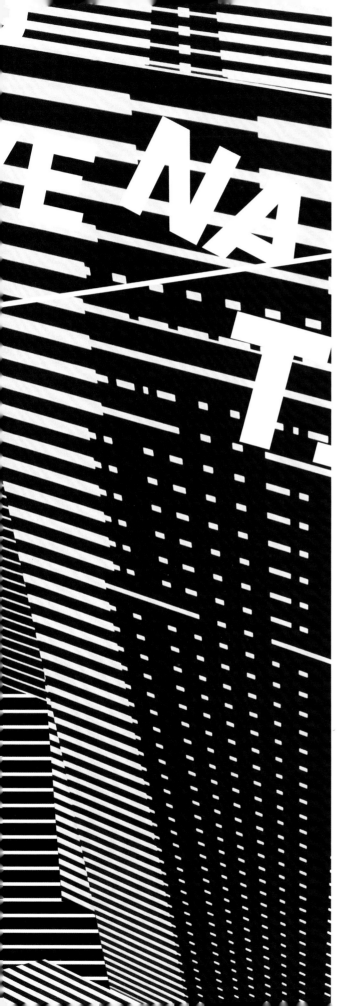

Making the Firebird Suite poster (p. 39) was another. I had found a lot of feathers at the hobby store, but I didn't really know what to do with them. You came up with a plan to place them in a 4 × 5 negative carrier and make images by projecting them in an enlarger onto high-contrast paper. We then sliced our favorite image and reassembled it to make the final feather (p. 40). Those were important experiments, and you never looked for obstacles, only for possibilities.

I remember drawing the Berkeley Typographers poster (p. 48). Initially, it was all done with pen and ink, but you encouraged using airbrushed areas to create a sense of "photographic space," with shaded areas to move the eye across the page.

I agree with you about the significance of the Honoring Matthew Carter poster (p. 182). I think it almost operates as a key to our entire body of work because it's about looking through a lens at graphic design. For me that poster sums up everything that we've tried to do.

I also remember that whenever I would travel to New York, I would go to MoMA to sit and stare at Picasso's *Les Demoiselles d'Avignon* (1907). Each time, I'd understand more about it. The first time I saw the painting, the gestures on the canvas appeared very random, and the logic didn't register at all, but after decades of visiting it, it gradually began to seem like hyperrealism.

T   The most interesting experience I remember with you in an art museum was when we went to see the constructivist exhibition, *The Great Utopia,* at the Guggenheim Museum in

Yale Symphony Orchestra,
Organizational Meeting
Poster, 1978, diazo print,
40 × 18 in.

the early '90s. You walked in and immediately looked shocked. It reminded me of our trip to the Chicago Field Museum, when we entered the mammal room, with its wall of skulls in various shapes and sizes. You had a similar look and said in a surprised voice, "I'm a mammal!" Your expression at the Guggenheim was very similar only this time your face exclaimed, "I'm a constructivist!" [both laugh]

N   I'm thinking about a term you invented, "bag of regret," to describe the disappointment that gets taken from one project to the next. I have to ask, what's your biggest "bag of regret" so far?

T   The "bag of regret" happens with every project. I can't think of one that didn't end up with at least a small "bag of regret." Sometimes the bag is small and sometimes it's very burdensome. It's as if there's always something you look at and say, "We could have done that better."

N   It really shouldn't be regrettable at all because it leads to progress. My freshman design teacher, Forrest Dahl, always said a good failure is worth a hundred mediocre successes.

T   It's also true that you can't expect to learn everything in one project, you gain what you can and move on to the next, you could call it "the bag of progress." That's why the process of making the work is so absorbing and rewarding. It's a very satisfying cycle and one we hope never ends.

Yale Symphony Orchestra,
Organizational Meeting
Poster (detail), 1978

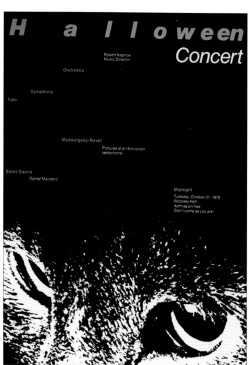

Yale Symphony Orchestra,
Halloween Poster, 1978,
offset lithograph,
32 × 20 in.

Philharmonia Orchestra
of Yale, Hindemith,
"Symphonie, Die Harmonie
der Welt" Poster, 1979,
offset lithograph, 30 × 20 in.

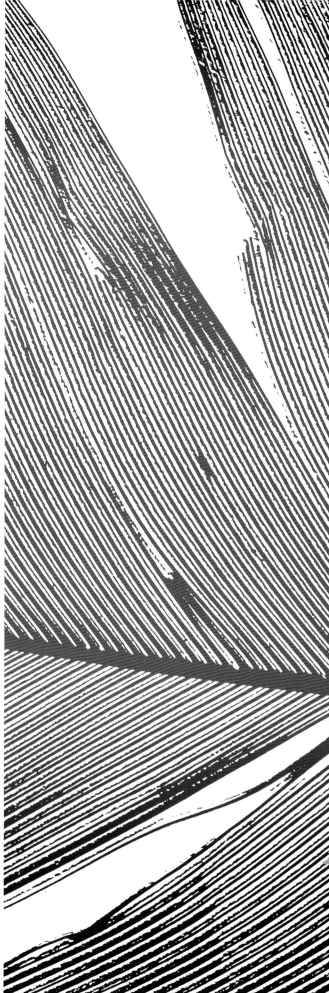

Yale Symphony Orchestra,
Firebird Suite Poster
(detail, the split fountain
made with one pass
through the press, inks
blended by the roller), 1978

Yale Symphony Orchestra,
Firebird Suite Poster, 1978,
offset lithograph, 32 × 20 in.

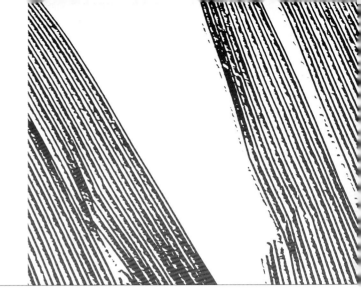

Yale Symphony Orchestra,
Firebird Suite Poster (in
process, realignment of
feather), 1978

Boston Acoustics, A200
Loudspeaker Poster and
Brochure (detail from photo
shoot), 1979

Boston Acoustics, A200
Loudspeaker Brochure, 1979,
offset lithograph, 11 × 7 in.

Boston Acoustics, A200 Loudspeaker Poster and Brochure (in process, photo shoot showing speaker drivers multiply exposed at various distances from the camera to illustrate sound), 1979

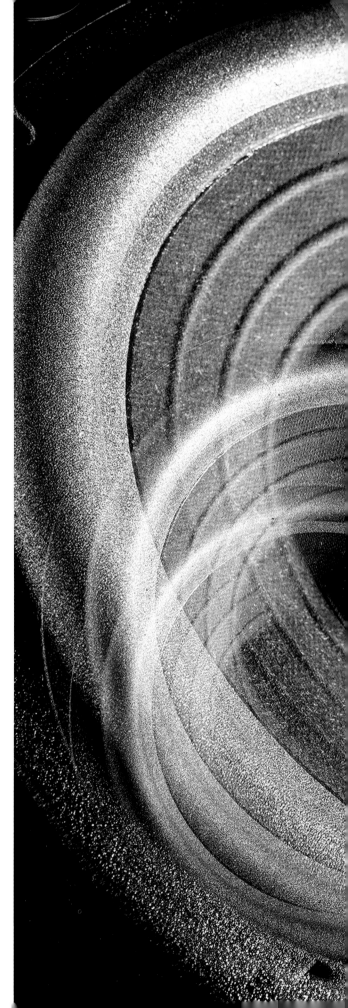

Boston Acoustics, A200
Loudspeaker Poster, 1979,
offset lithograph, 30 × 21 in.

<u>1983</u> Crystal Chair wins a *Progressive Architecture* International Furniture Competition Award

<u>1983</u> Crystal Chair is featured in *New York Times,* "Prize Winning Designs"

<u>1983</u> Studio is featured in *IDEA* magazine, Japan

<u>1984</u> Skolos is Panelist for Cooper Hewitt, "Directions in Graphic Design: A Survey of New Work"

<u>1985</u> Studio moves to the Schrafft Building in Charlestown, MA

<u>1985</u> Berkeley Typographers poster is included in *Image des Mots,* Centre Georges Pompidou, Paris

<u>1985</u> ALL-IN-1 poster receives the Silver Prize in the *Lahti Poster Biennial,* Finland

<u>1986</u> Wedell speaks at the Industrial Design Society of America (IDSA) Conference, "Forms of Design"

<u>1988</u> Studio is featured in *New American Design*— Hugh Aldersey- Williams, Rizzoli

<u>1988</u> Delphax Fonts poster is included in *The Modern Poster,* Museum of Modern Art, New York

<u>1988</u> ALL-IN-1 poster receives the Bronze Medal in the *International Triennial of Posters,* Toyama, Japan

<u>1989</u> Skolos begins adjunct teaching at the Rhode Island School of Design

<u>1989</u> Berkeley Typographers poster is included in *Graphic Design in America,* Walker Art Center, Minneapolis

44

'80s: Photography
Finds Design

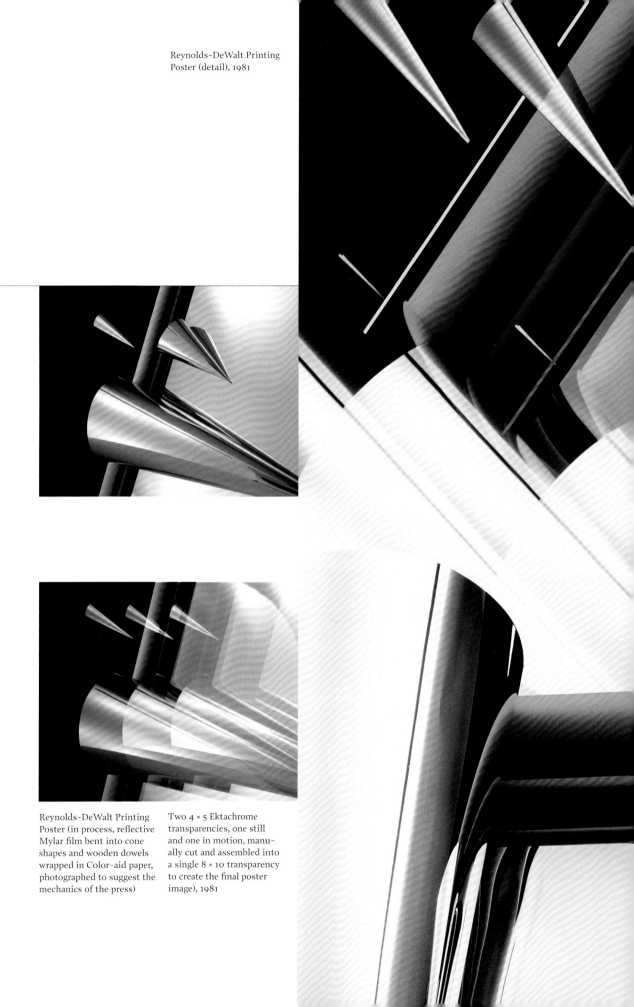

Reynolds-DeWalt Printing
Poster (detail), 1981

Reynolds-DeWalt Printing
Poster (in process, reflective
Mylar film bent into cone
shapes and wooden dowels
wrapped in Color-aid paper,
photographed to suggest the
mechanics of the press)

Two 4 × 5 Ektachrome
transparencies, one still
and one in motion, manu-
ally cut and assembled into
a single 8 × 10 transparency
to create the final poster
image), 1981

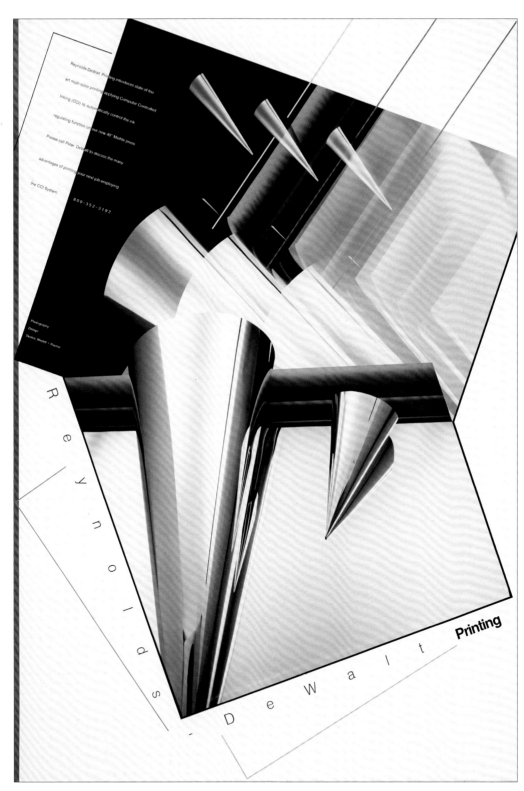

Reynolds-DeWalt Printing
Poster, 1981, offset
lithograph, 33 × 21 in.

A De Stijl–influenced approach to composition and color informed a sequence of three posters for Berkeley Typographers based on the geometry of the letter *B*.

Berkeley Typographers Poster (in process, paper and Rapidograph mock-up, 4 × 4 in.), 1981

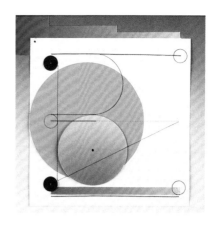

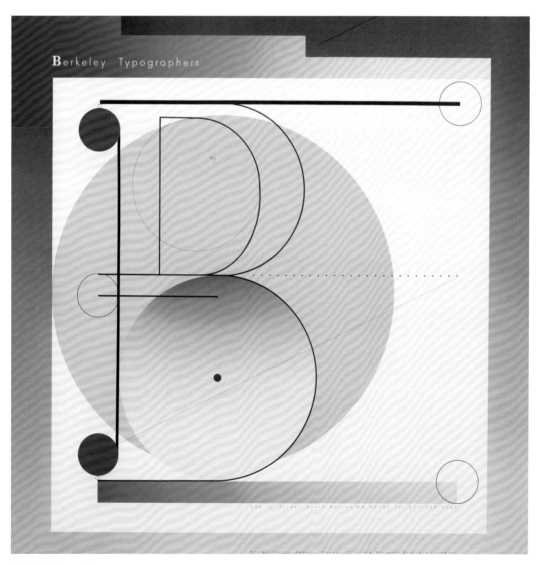

Berkeley Typographers Poster, 1981, offset lithograph, 25 × 25 in.

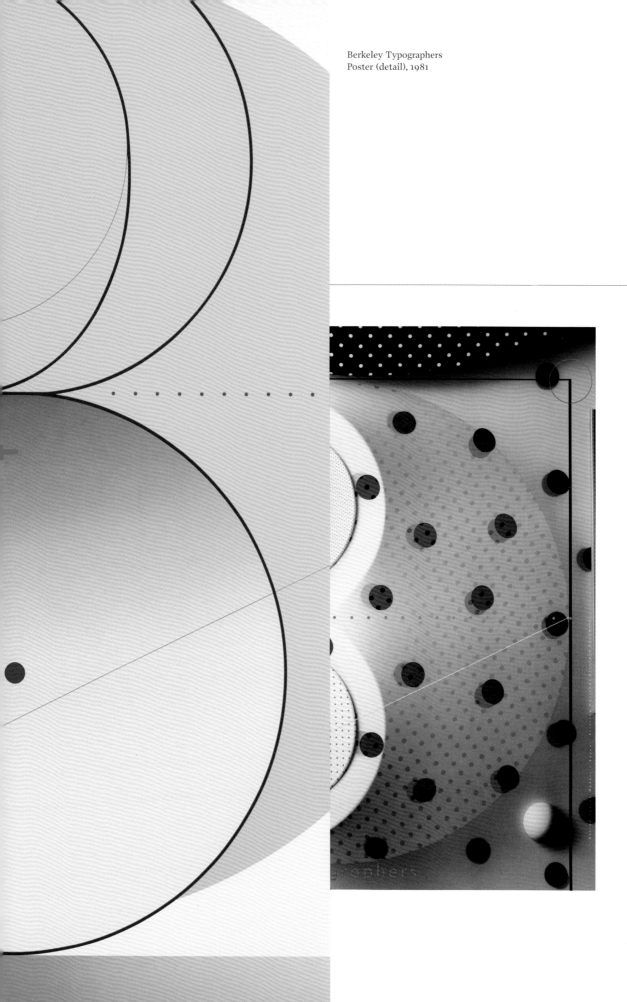

Berkeley Typographers
Poster (detail), 1981

Berkeley Typographers

Berkeley Typographers
Poster (detail), 1981

For the second Berkeley
Typographers Poster,
1986, the letter *B* was
constructed from a variety
of polka dot fabrics applied
to geometric forms, with
overlapping fabric and
multiple exposures creating
an illusion of layering.

Berkeley Typographers
Poster, 1986, offset
lithograph, 25 × 25 in.

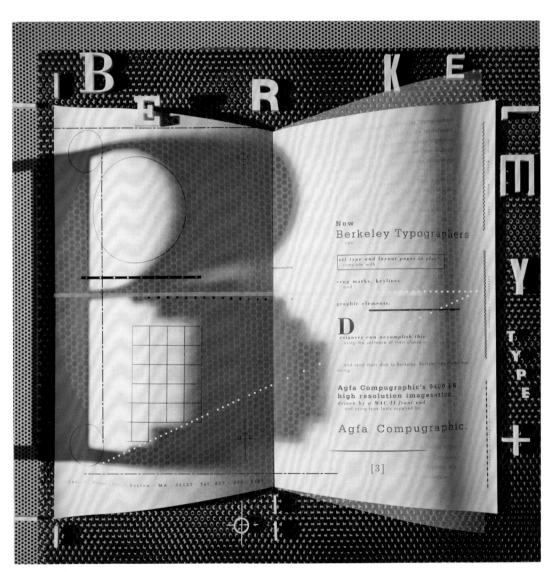

Berkeley Typographers
Poster, 1989, offset
lithograph, 25 × 25 in.

Skolos, Wedell + Raynor • 1989

Separations • Laserscan, Inc.

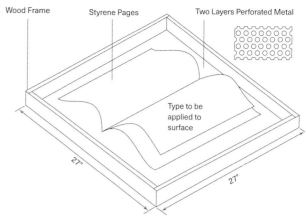

Wood Frame   Styrene Pages   Two Layers Perforated Metal

Type to be
applied to
surface

27"

27"

Top: Berkeley Typographers
Poster (in process, model
assembly instructions for
fabricating styrene book on a
perforated metal base), 1989

Berkeley Typographers
Poster (in process, model
photoshoot), 1989

Berkeley Typographers
Poster (detail), 1989

Digital Equipment Corporation, ALL-IN-1 Poster, "Information Systems that Grow with You," (in process, material, paint, and background tests), 1983

Right: Chambered nautilus shell painted flat white on cool background

Below: Chambered nautilus shell unpainted on warm background

Digital Equipment
Corporation, ALL-IN-1
Poster (detail), 1983

Digital Equipment
Corporation, ALL-IN-1
Poster (detail), 1983

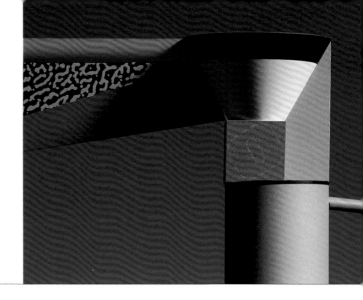

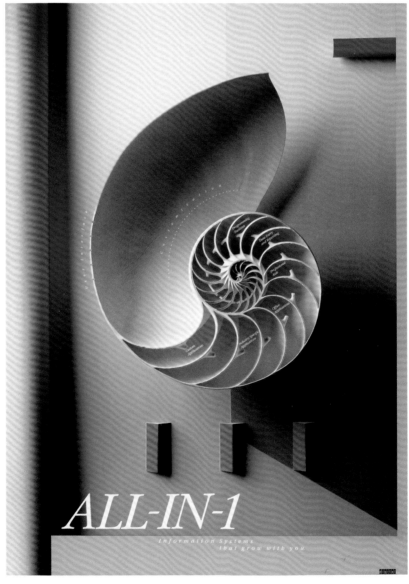

Digital Equipment
Corporation ALL-IN-1 Poster,
"Information Systems that
Grow with You," 1983, offset
lithograph, 32 × 26 in.

For the Olivetti Peripherals Graphic Identity Poster (designed in collaboration with Larry Yang), 1984, a negative of the dotted Olivetti o was pushed to the edges of the frame to represent Olivetti's peripheral products, such as tractor-feed printers and printer ribbons, then backlit and exposed with four colored gels and thrown out of focus to create progressive degrees of glow. The model and logos were shot separately as 8 × 10 Ektachrome transparencies and manually cut and inlaid by a photo retoucher.

Opposite: scale model construction of Memphis Group—inspired frame, painted and paper-covered Plexiglas with transfer graphics, approx. 12 × 8 in.

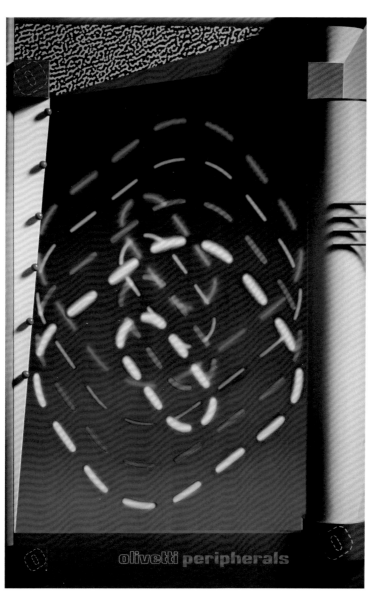

Olivetti Peripherals Poster, 1984, offset lithograph, 36 × 23½ in.

AIGA Boston, Pentagram
Lecture Poster, 1984, offset
lithograph, 36 × 23 in.

Inspired by the 1985 arrival of Haley's Comet, star maps became the backdrop for a diagrammatic interpretation of projection television technology for Kloss Video Corporation.

The RGB cathode ray tubes represented by semicircles in the lower right corner of the poster reflect and bounce the light through the poster space and onto the screen in the opposite corner.

Kloss Video Corporation,
Videobeam Poster, 1985,
offset lithograph, 36 × 36 in.

Kloss Video Corporation, Videobeam Poster (in process, tracing paper grids and colored paper mock-ups with Letraset geometric elements), 5 × 5 in.

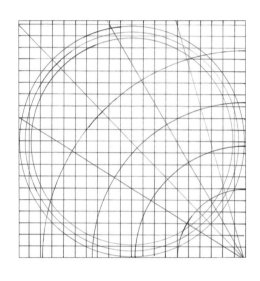

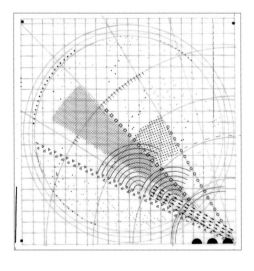

Skolos, Wedell + Raynor,
Stationery, 1979, one-color
offset lithograph

Skolos, Wedell + Raynor,
Stationery, 1982, three-color
offset lithograph

Skolos, Wedell + Raynor,
Stationery (detail), 1985

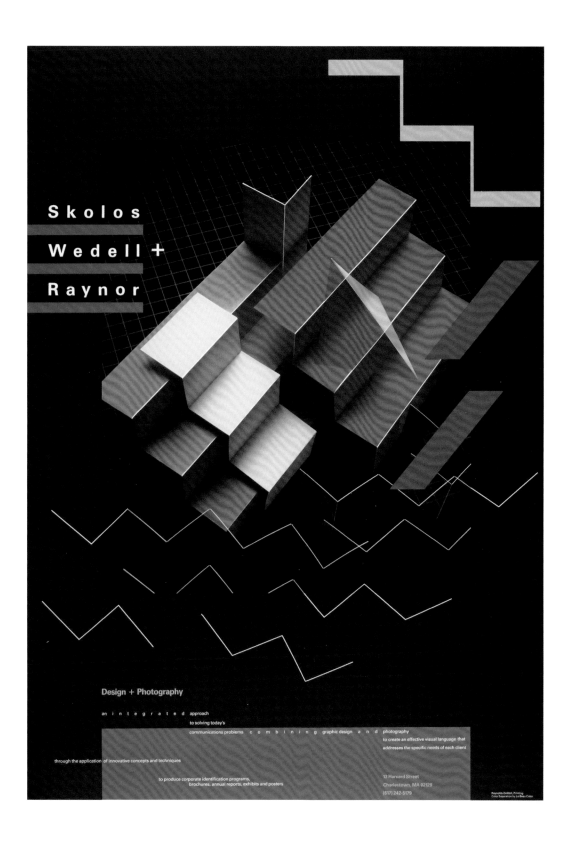

Skolos, Wedell + Raynor,
Stationery, 1985, four-color
(spot) offset lithograph
with die cut and emboss

Skolos-Wedell, Stationery,
1990, two-color offset
lithograph and emboss

Skolos-Wedell, Stationery,
1996, two-color offset
lithograph

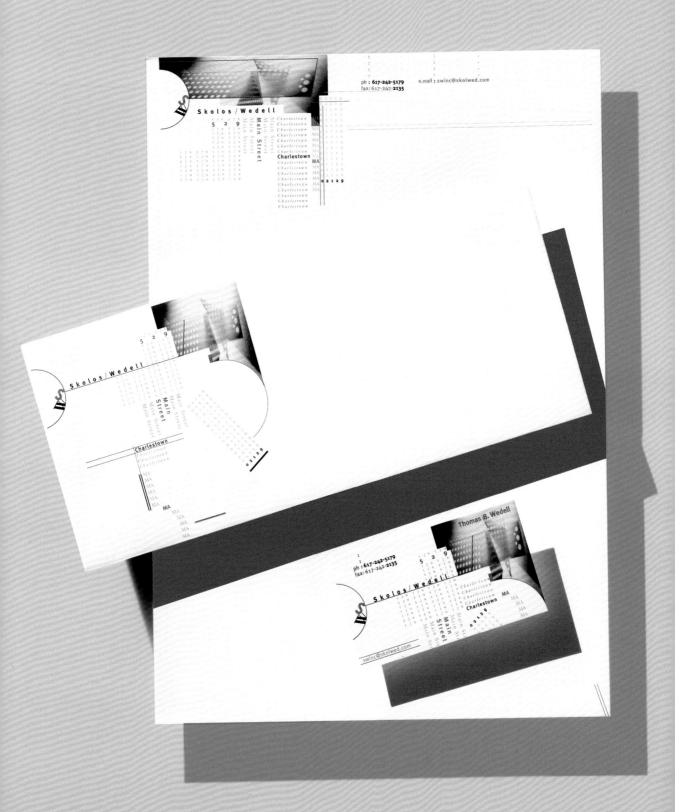

Skolos-Wedell, Stationery,
2000, three-color offset
lithograph

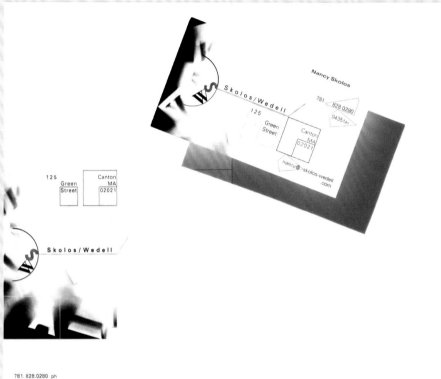

For the Delphax Fonts Poster, 1987, model materials included sparkly fabric, graduated paper, textured rubber sheet, jigsaw-cut Plexiglas letters, and geometric solids sprayed with metallic paint. The metallic quality of the image was preserved by converting it to a metallic copper and black duotone for printing.

Opposite: Delphax Fonts Poster (detail), 1987

ion

page

printing

Delphax Fonts Poster (in process, colored paper compositional sketch), 1987

The poster highlighted Delphax's high-speed ion-technology and diagrammed the process of rendering the type by pushing negatively charged toner through a matrix and onto a positively charged drum, fusing the type onto the paper.

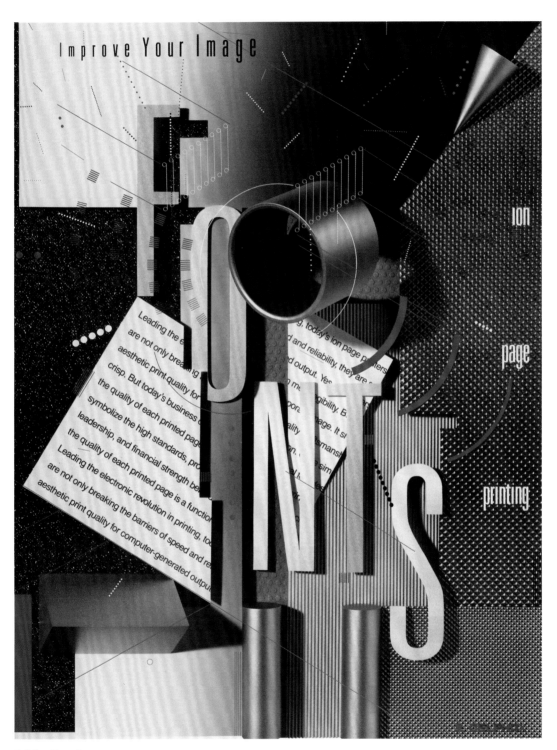

Delphax Fonts Poster,
1987, offset lithograph,
44 × 33 in.

Graphic Identity for
Archetype Architecture,
Joel Bargmann and
Jonathan Leffell, Architects,
1987, adapted forms and
surfaces from the firm's
postmodern aesthetic.

Opposite: Archetype
Architecture, Brochure,
offset lithograph, accordion
fold (folds to fit in a 9 × 12
in. envelope), 1987

Archetype
Architecture, Inc.

Archetype Architecture
Stationery, 1987, two-color
offset lithograph with die cut

Opposite: Archetype
Architecture Brochure
(interior), 1987

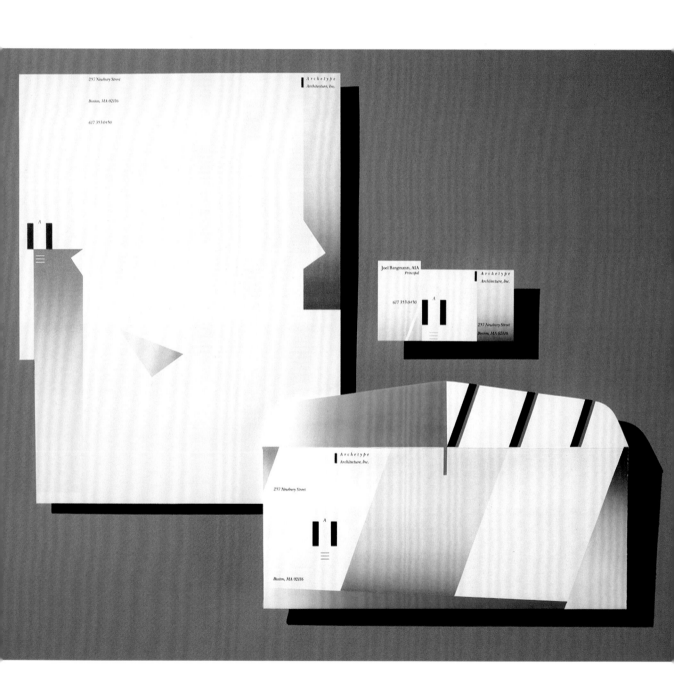

Megaphone Chair, 1988, Plexiglas and sheet metal, scale model: 1 in. = 1 ft. (*Progressive Architecture* magazine, Conceptual Furniture Design Competition Entry; *ID* magazine Annual Design Review Honorable Mention)

Influenced by Russian constructivist propaganda stands, the Megaphone Chair required its user to sit on two flattened megaphones that embodied uncomfortable postmodern ideas.

Megaphone Chair (in process,
the chair's silhouette
emerged when a scrap
fell away from one of the
invitation mock-ups), 1988

Symmes, Maini & McKee,
Associates, Inc., 30th
Anniversary Invitation, 1988,
two-color offset lithograph
with die cut, 9 × 4 in.

architectu

Symmes
Maini &
McKee
Associates, Inc.

30TH

YEAR

structural engineering

architecture

interior design

Symmes
Maini &
McKee
Associates, Inc.

30TH

YEAR

structural engineering

electrical engineering

plumbing engineering

site planning

SBK Entertainment World
Identity and Poster, 1988
offset lithograph, 36 × 26 in.

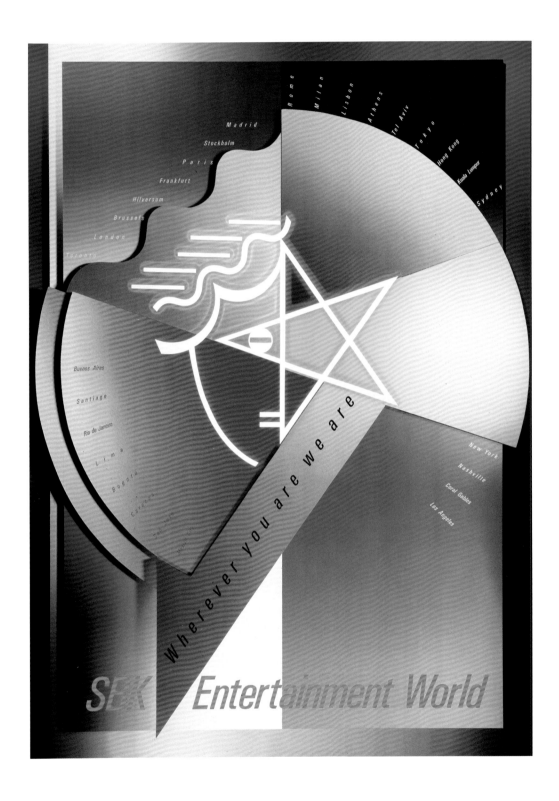

SBK Entertainment World
Identity and Poster, 1989
offset lithograph, 36 × 26 in.

Swid Powell Stationery
(detail), 1987

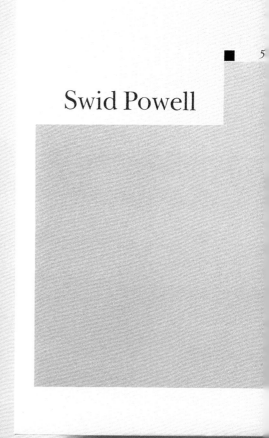

Swid Powell

Swid Powell Stationery,
1987, two-color offset
lithograph with die cut

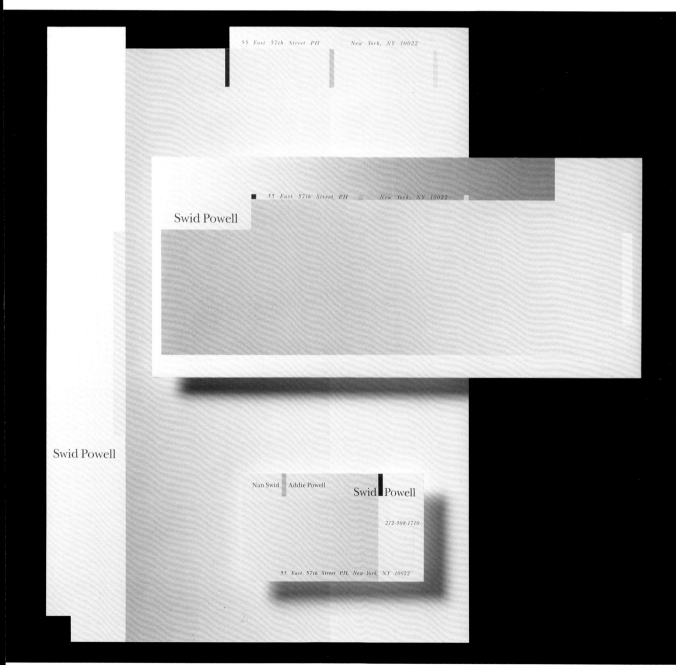

Swid Powell Brochure for
architect-designed tableware,
1988, offset lithograph,
nine-panel accordion fold,
angled trim top, folds to
10 ½ × 5 ½ in.

Laserscan Poster (detail),
1989, offset lithograph with
die cut, 36 × 21 ½ in.

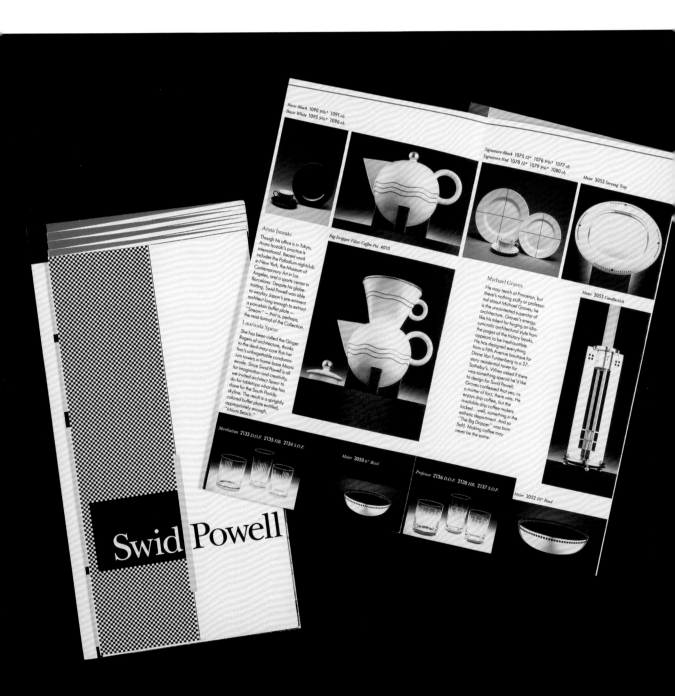

Laserscan Poster (in process, 4 × 5 and 2 ¼ color transparencies digitally drum scanned, and assembled with Quantel Paintbox to showcase its capabilities), 1989

Laserscan Poster, 1989,
offset lithograph with die
cut, 36 × 21 ½ in.

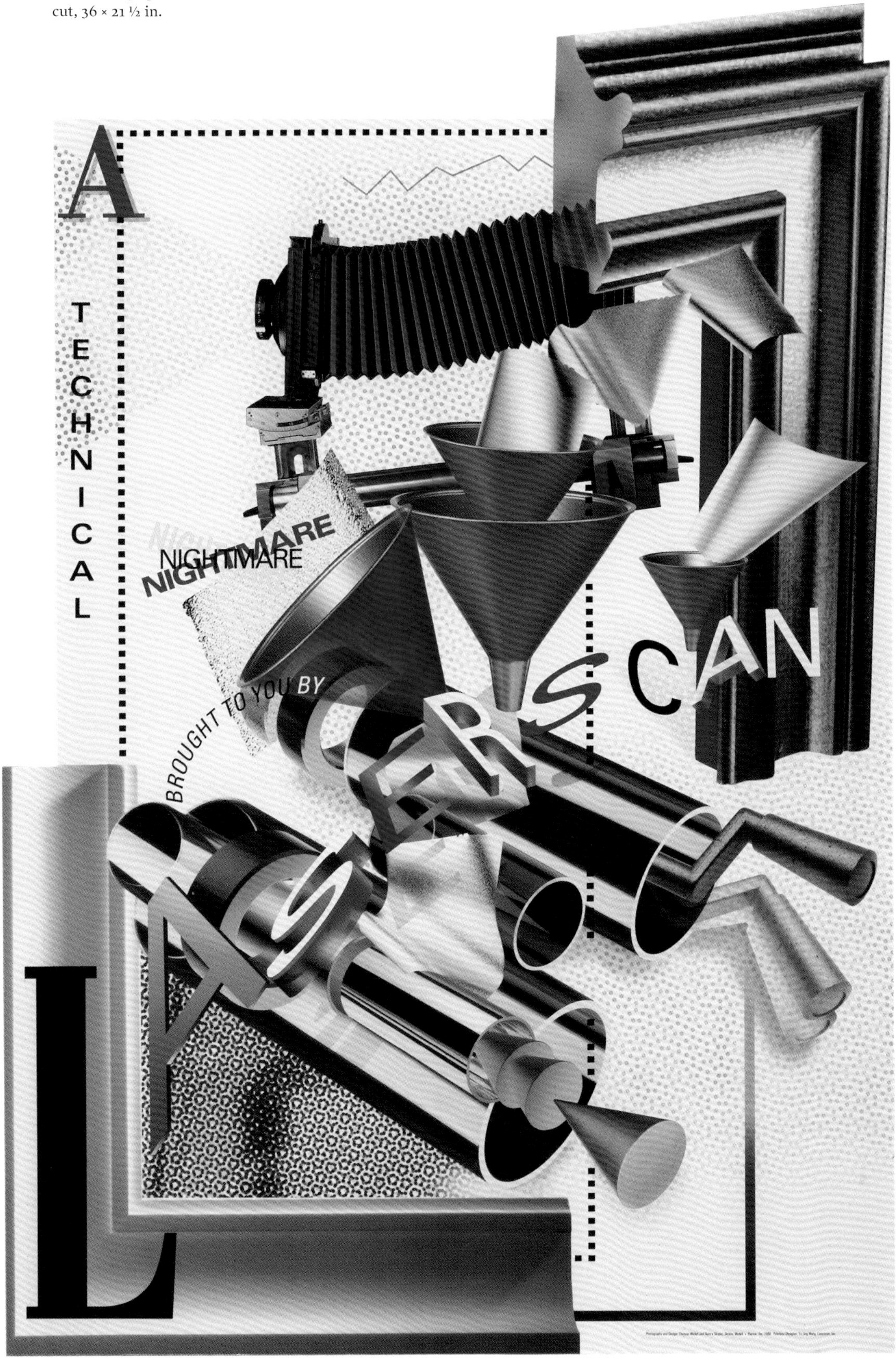

1990 Studio featured in *Communication Arts*, "Skolos, Wedell and Raynor"

1990 Raynor and family move back to Michigan and studio becomes Skolos-Wedell

1992 Poster included in *30 Posters on the Environment and Development*, Museum of Modern Art, Rio de Janeiro

1992–95 Skolos and Wedell are Visiting Critics at Yale

1993 Wedell begins adjunct teaching at RISD

1993 Studio is profiled in *Creation 15*, "Skolos-Wedell," Japan

1993 *Ferrington Guitars* is featured in *Graphis 284*, "Bringing Guitars to Life"

1993 Studio is profiled in *Eye No. 8 Vol. 2*, "Techno Cubists"

1996 Studio designs *Computer Technology* stamp

1996 Skolos-Wedell has solo show, *2d/3d Fusion*, Creation Gallery, Tokyo

1996 Work included in *Mixing Messages*, Cooper Hewitt National Design Museum, New York

1997 Studio has solo show, *Skolos-Wedell*, Schüle für Gestaltung, Basel

1998 Skolos is elected to AGI

1999 Skolos becomes a full-time Associate Professor of Graphic Design at RISD

1999 Jon McKee and Mark Hutker design Skolos-Wedell's home and studio, Canton, MA

'90s: Postmodern
Complexity

Opposite: Lyceum Fellowship, Student Architecture Competition Poster, 1990, offset lithograph, 32 × 20 in.

The 1990 program called for the design of a water treatment plant in Boston Harbor.

Right: Compositional scenarios discovered in flat file paper drawers

Below: Lyceum Fellowship Poster (in process, sketch made from color paper scraps), 1990

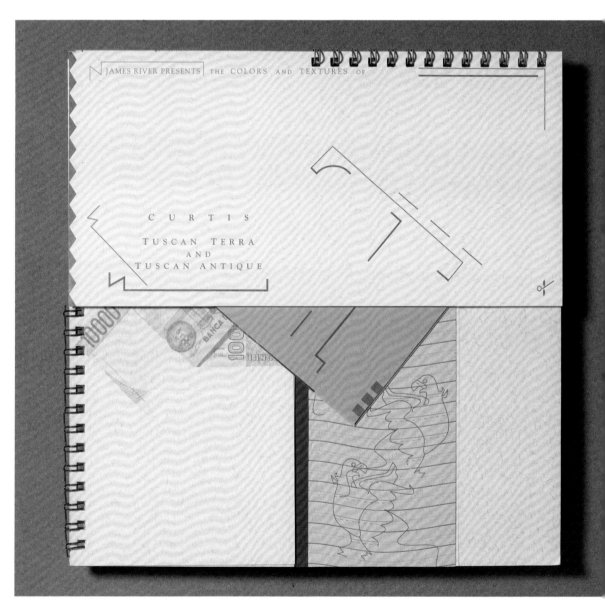

James River Paper, Curtis,
"Tuscan Terra" and "Tuscan
Antique" Paper Promotion,
1990, offset lithograph,
wire bound, 8 × 8 in.

Tuscan-themed miniature
landscapes created in the
photo studio were incorporated into the booklet.

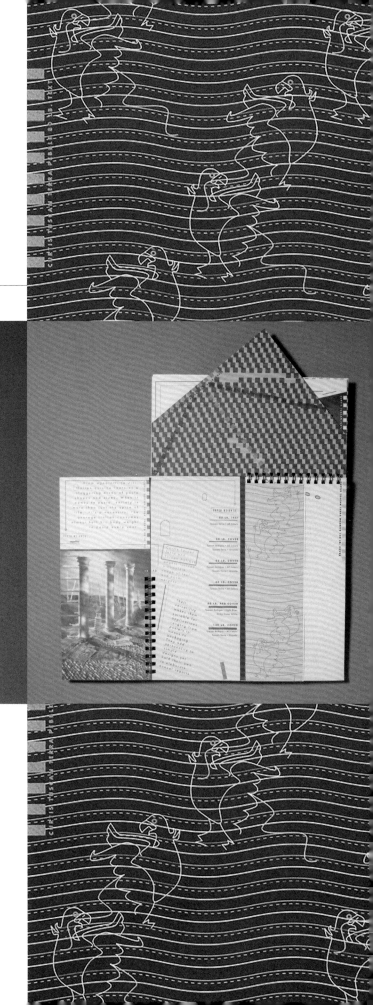

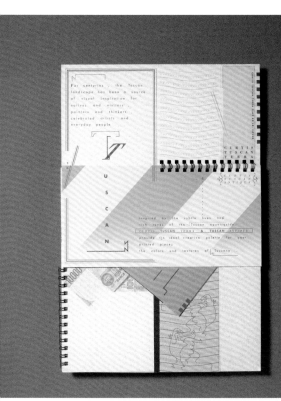

The binding allowed the
papers to interact as
swatches showing spot
colors, halftones, duotones,
four-color printing,
thermography, and foil
stamping.

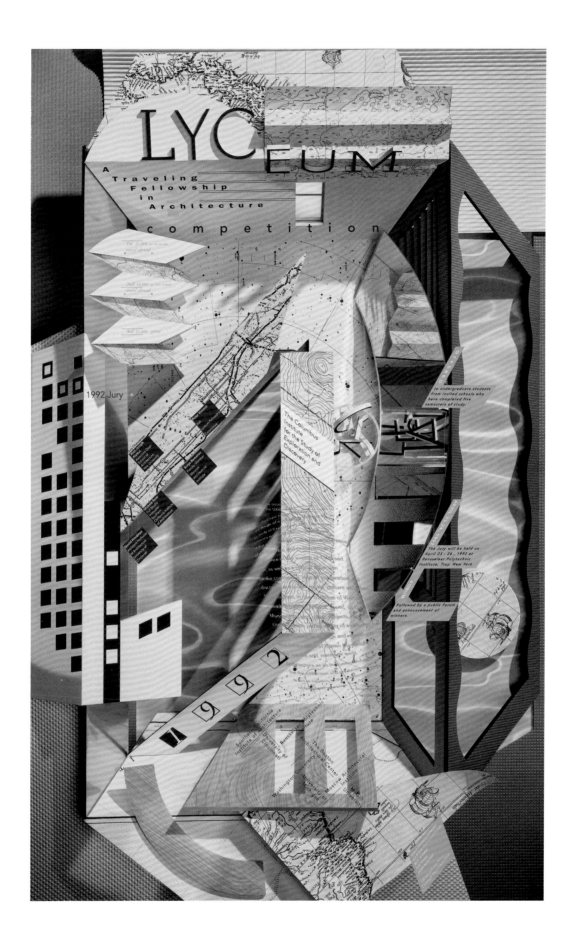

Within the poster image (detail):

PRIZES:

1ST : $7,000
& SIX MONTHS
TRAVEL ABROAD

2ND : $4,000
THREE MONTHS
TRAVEL ABROAD

3RD : $1,000
GRANT

ALTERNATE :
CITATION

Lyceum
Fellowship Committee

Jon McKee,
Chairman and Founder
Mark A. Hutker
Peter Vincent
Steven Arons
Joseph Sziabowski

1000 Massachusetts Ave
Cambridge, Massachusetts 02138

Opposite: Lyceum Fellow-
ship, Student Architecture
Competition Poster, 1992,
offset lithograph, 32 × 20 in.

Lyceum Fellowship Poster
(detail), 1992

The 1992 program called
for the design of a library
and map room. The photo-
graphic model was designed
with openings strategically
positioned to shape light
and shadows.

Lyceum Fellowship, Student
Architecture Competition
Poster, 1991, offset
lithograph, 20 × 32 in.

The 1991 program called
for the design of a bicycle
factory in Mexico City.

The Cooper Union

Rensselaer Polytechnic Institute

Southern California Institute of Architecture

University of

91

TRAVELING FELLOWSHIP

PRIZES:

1ST : $7,000
FOR SIX MONTHS
TRAVEL ABROAD

2ND : $4,000
FOR THREE MONTHS
TRAVEL ABROAD

3RD : $1,000
GRANT

ALTERNATE :
CITATION

Lyceum
Fellowship Committee

Jon McKee,
Chairman and Founder
Mark A. Hutker
Peter Vincent
Steven Arens
Joseph Szlabowski

1000 Massachusetts Ave.
Cambridge, Massachusetts 02138

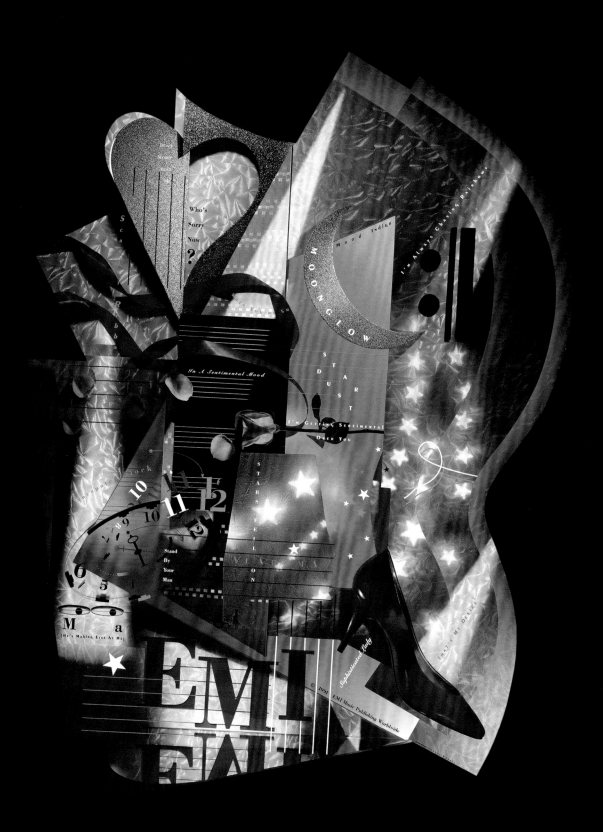

Opposite: EMI Music,
1930s Song Catalog Poster,
1991, offset lithograph, die-
cut, 39 × 27 in.

Lyceum Fellowship,
Student Architecture
Competition Poster, 1993,
offset lithograph,
32 × 20 in.

Lyceum Fellowship Poster
(detail), 1993

The 1993 program called
for the design of a music
school mixing the study of
classical and blues music.

Neocon 23 Poster
(in process, sketch
made from color paper
scraps), 1991

Neocon 23 Poster (in
process, photo shoot
set-up of layered, painted,
and vinyl-covered
Plexiglas surfaces and
jigsaw-cut letters, colored
details applied with
transfer graphics), 1991

Neocon 23 Poster
(detail), 1991

Neocon 23 Poster, 1991,
offset lithograph, 36 × 24 in.

Opposite: *Ferrington Guitars,* Callaway Editions, 1992, offset lithography, 13 ½ × 10 in.

The book's asymmetric shape naturally evolved as a reaction to the off-center shapes and angular forms of Danny Ferrington's guitars. Multiple views of his dynamic guitar designs were easy to arrange within the trapezoidal spreads.

Ferrington Guitars (in process, cover photo shoot with fragmented guitar shapes fabricated by Ferrington, surrounding one of his fully built guitars), 1992

Ferrington Guitars
(process image of photo
shoot), 1992

44

A compact disk of the book's guitars being played was housed in a die-cut, recessed circle in the cover's book board.

Photography was the first step in the design process. Luthier Danny Ferrington supervised the initial photo shoots, holding the guitars up at every angle as we attached Post-it notes with reminders of the best views. Because guitars have no particular orientation, photographs could be taken from any angle.

Ferrington Guitars (in process, Nancy and Tom sequencing spreads), 1992

The guitars arrived at the studio in small batches as they were available, so the order of the book was in a constant state of flux.

We were fortunate to get access and support from Kodak's Center for Creative Imaging in Camden, Maine, where we used Kodak's Premier Image Enhancement System to assemble the double-page layouts which were too large to produce at the time on desktop computer systems.

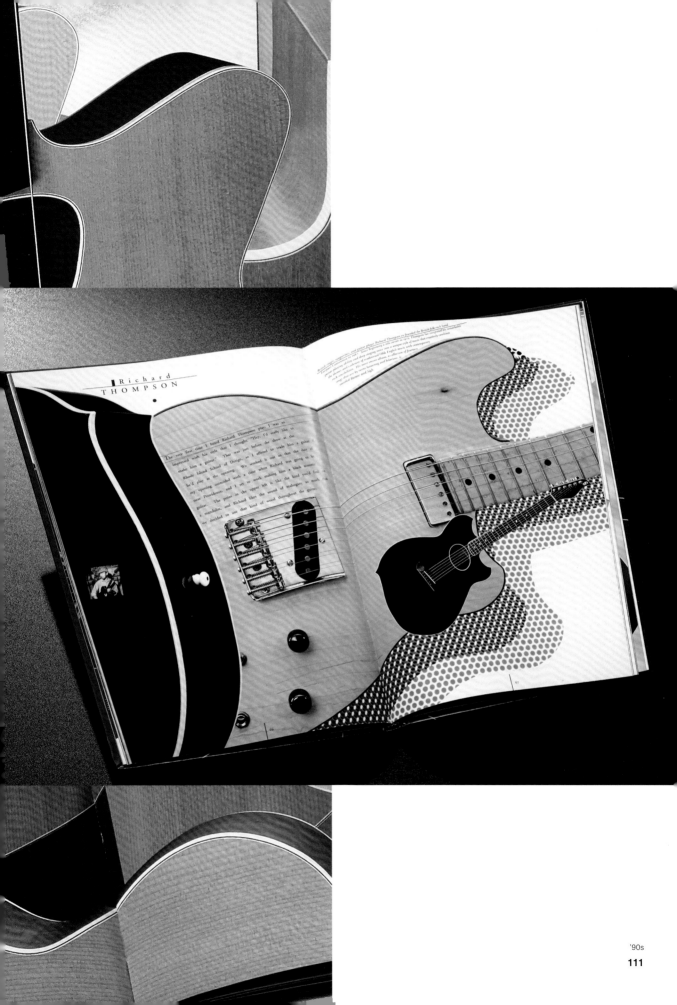

3. Woods are joined for the top (or soundboard) and back. The edges to be joined are first sanded smooth, and then glued together and tied into an old-fashioned rope clamp, so the joint will be even and secure. This guitar will have a spruce top and a mahogany back.

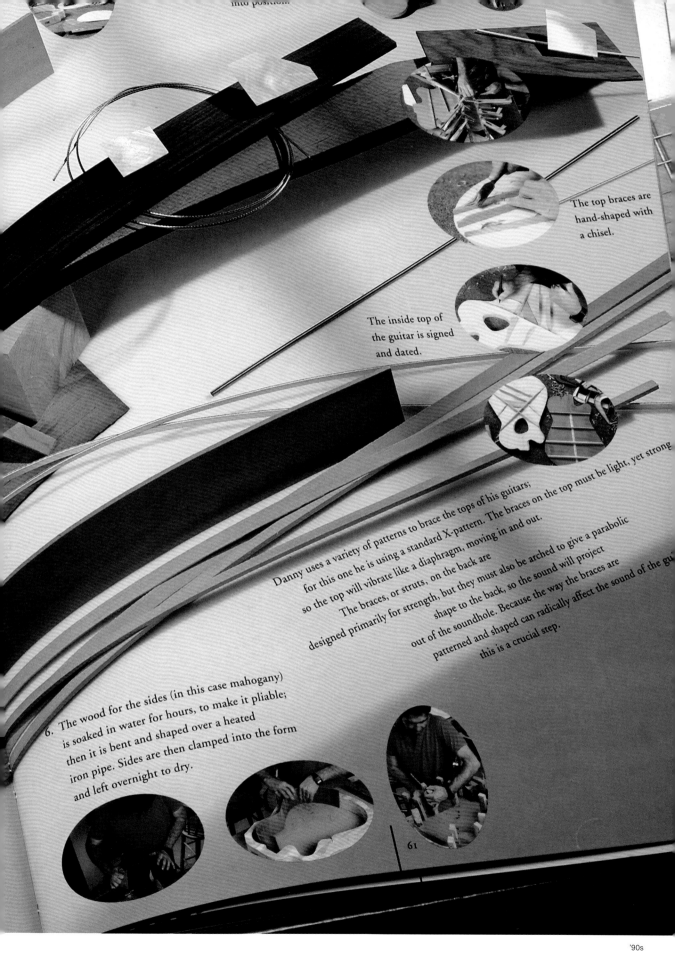

The top braces are hand-shaped with a chisel.

The inside top of the guitar is signed and dated.

Danny uses a variety of patterns to brace the tops of his guitars; for this one he is using a standard X-pattern. The braces on the top must be light, yet strong so the top will vibrate like a diaphragm, moving in and out.

The braces, or struts, on the back are designed primarily for strength, but they must also be arched to give a parabolic shape to the back, so the sound will project out of the soundhole. Because the way the braces are patterned and shaped can radically affect the sound of the gui this is a crucial step.

6. The wood for the sides (in this case mahogany) is soaked in water for hours, to make it pliable; then it is bent and shaped over a heated iron pipe. Sides are then clamped into the form and left overnight to dry.

61

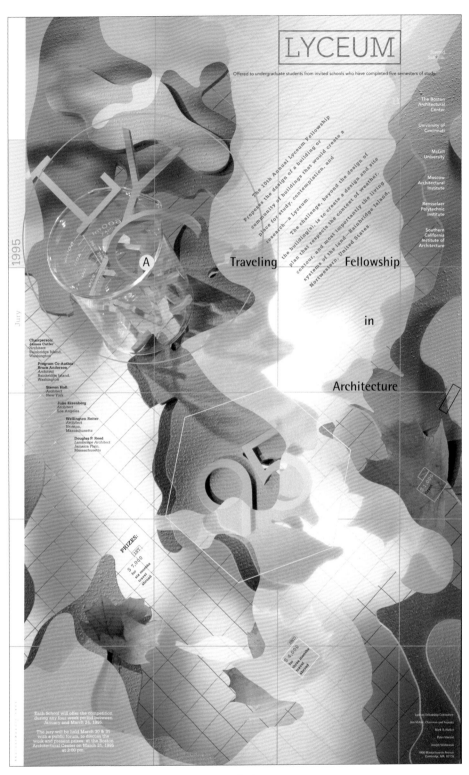

LYCEUM

Offered to undergraduate students from invited schools who have completed five semesters of study.

The 10th Annual Lyceum Fellowship Proposes the design of a building or community of buildings that would create a place for study, contemplation, and research...a Lyceum.

The challenge, beyond the design of the building(s), is to create a design and site plan that respects the context of weather, contour, and most importantly the living systems of the land—Bainbridge Island, Nortwestern, United States.

Traveling   Fellowship

in

Architecture

1995

Jury

Chairperson:
James Cutler
Architect
Bainbridge Island,
Washington

Program Co-Author:
Bruce Anderson
Architect
Bainbridge Island,
Washington

Steven Holl
Architect
New York

Julie Eizenberg
Architect
Los Angeles

Wellington Reiter
Architect
Newton,
Massachusetts

Douglas P. Reed
Landscape Architect
Jamaica Plain,
Massachusetts

PRIZES:
1ST
$ 7,000
for
six months
travel
abroad

2ND
$ 4,000
for
three months
travel
abroad

The Boston
Architectural
Center

University of
Cincinnati

McGill
University

Moscow
Architectural
Institute

Rensselaer
Polytechnic
Institute

Southern
California
Institute of
Architecture

Each School will offer the competition during any four week period between January and March 24, 1995.

The jury will be held March 30 & 31 with a public forum, to discuss the work and present prizes, at the Boston Architectural Center on March 31, 1995 at 2:00 pm

Lyceum Fellowship Committee

Jon McKee, Chairman and Founder

Mark A. Hutker

Peter Vanze

Jerold Milatowski

1000 Massachusetts Avenue
Cambridge, MA 02138

Lyceum Fellowship, Student
Architecture Competition
Poster, 1995, offset
lithograph, 32 × 20 in.

The 1995 program examined
the weather and ecology
of Bainbridge Island as a
context for architecture.

Lyceum Fellowship, Student
Architecture Competition
Poster (detail), 1996

Maine College of Art, Summer
Institute in Graphic Design
Poster, 1996, offset lithograph,
42 ½ × 31 ¼ in.

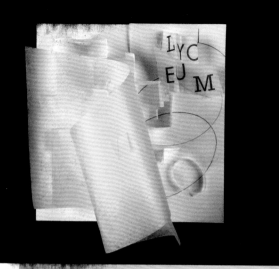

Lyceum Fellowship, Student Architecture Competition Poster (in process, preliminary paper model), 1996, yellow trace and Bristol board, 5 × 5 in.

The design for the 1996 poster focused on architects' ideation tools to illustrate the program, which advocated for architects' skills in home design.

Lyceum Fellowship, Student Architecture Competition Poster, 1996, offset lithograph on vellum, 26 × 26 in.

Documenting Marcel
Exhibition Poster (detail),
1996

Below: United States
Postal Service, Computer
Technology Stamp (detail
of cube photo set-up,
which reappeared in the
Duchamp photo shoot),
1996

Opposite: *Documenting
Marcel* Exhibition Poster,
1996, offset lithography on
textured vellum, 36 × 24 in.

The exhibition at Reinhold-
Brown Gallery, New York,
featured promotional
ephemera from all of
Marcel Duchamp's known
gallery shows. The poster's
design was influenced by
Duchamp's 1953 poster
for a Dada exhibition at
Sidney Janis Gallery. It was
designed as a "cubist" chess
board with chess pieces
modeled after a design by
Man Ray.

m Haus Lange
Duchamp.

Musée de
Les Ducha
Jacques V
Duchamp-
Duchamp.
15 April–1
1967.

32.
Genoa.
Galleria d'A
Bertesca
Marc
Ju

17.
London. Gimpel Fils.
Marcel Duchamp.
December
–January

33.
Milan.
Galleria S
Marcel Du
dal 1902 a
7 Novemb
1967.

18.
Milan.
Galleria Schwarz.
Marcel Duchamp:
Ready-Mades, etc.
1964.

allery.

**20 October–18 December
1949.**

19.
**Bologna. Gavina.
Marcel Duchamp
ready-made.
June**
1965.

34.
Paris.
Musée Nation
Moderne.
Raym
Mar

20.
The Hague.
Haags Gemeentemuseum.
Marcel Duchamp:
Schilderijen, tekeningen,
ready-mades, documenten.
3 February–15
March 1965.

allery.

Art.

35.
Milan.
Biblioteca
The Large
Related W
7 Novemb
1967.

21.
Hannover

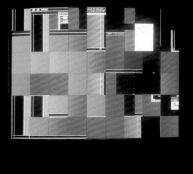

Opposite: United States Postal Service, Computer Technology Stamp, 1996, offset lithography and intaglio, $^{17}/_{16}$ × $^{11}/_{16}$ in.

A screensaver sparked the idea of a pixel-like structure for the Computer Technology Stamp, which commemorated the 50th anniversary of the computer's invention.

Lyceum Fellowship, Student
Architecture Competition
Poster (detail), 1997

The 1997 program called
for the design of a bird
sanctuary and observatory.

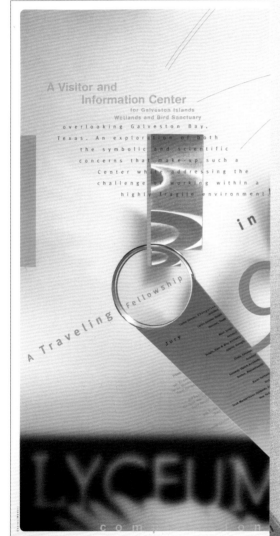

Skolos-Wedell, *2d−3d*
Fusion Exhibition Poster,
Creation G8 Gallery, Tokyo,
1996, offset lithograph,
40 × 29 in.

Lyceum Fellowship, Student Architecture Competition Poster, 1997, offset lithograph on watercolor paper, 26 × 26 in.

Lyceum Fellowship Poster (in process, assembly instructions for fabricating the photographic model with frosted Plexiglas layers, bird wing, and lenses amplifying the program's theme of bird watching), 1997

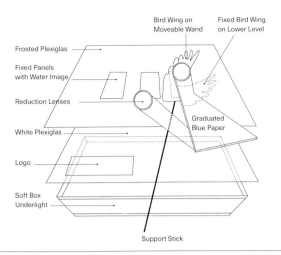

Frosted Plexiglas

Fixed Panels with Water Image

Reduction Lenses

White Plexiglas

Logo

Soft Box Underlight

Bird Wing on Moveable Wand

Fixed Bird Wing on Lower Level

Graduated Blue Paper

Support Stick

Lyceum Fellowship, Student
Architecture Competition
Poster (in process, the
magazine collage was scanned
into the computer and
developed into sketches with
bird and architecture imagery
reinforcing the program), 1997

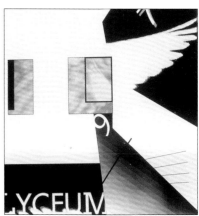

Lyceum Fellowship, Student
Architecture Competition
Poster (detail), 1999

The 1999 program called
for the design of an
internet museum.

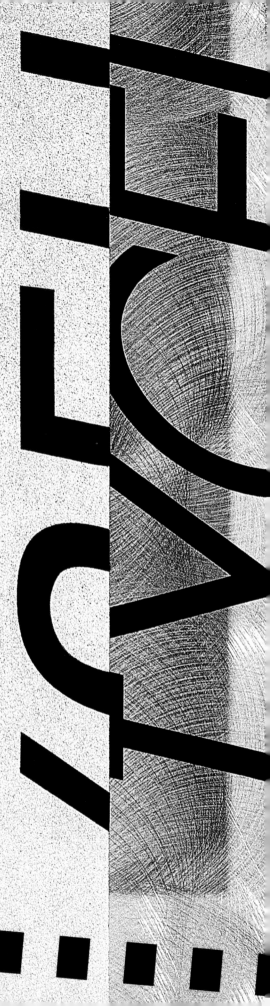

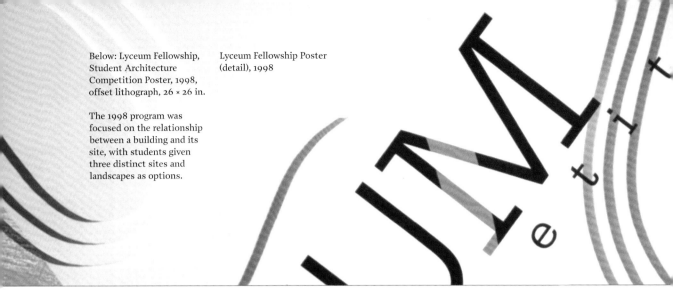

Below: Lyceum Fellowship, Student Architecture Competition Poster, 1998, offset lithograph, 26 × 26 in.

The 1998 program was focused on the relationship between a building and its site, with students given three distinct sites and landscapes as options.

Lyceum Fellowship Poster (detail), 1998

Lyceum Fellowship,
Student Architecture
Competition Poster,
1999, offset lithograph,
26 × 26 in.

Lyceum Fellowship Poster
(in process, collage), 1999

The hidden typographic
elements, wires, and
colored pixel/punch card
shapes in this collage
seemed a perfect fit for
the 1999 program that
asked students to design
a museum that would
embody the hidden nature
of the internet.

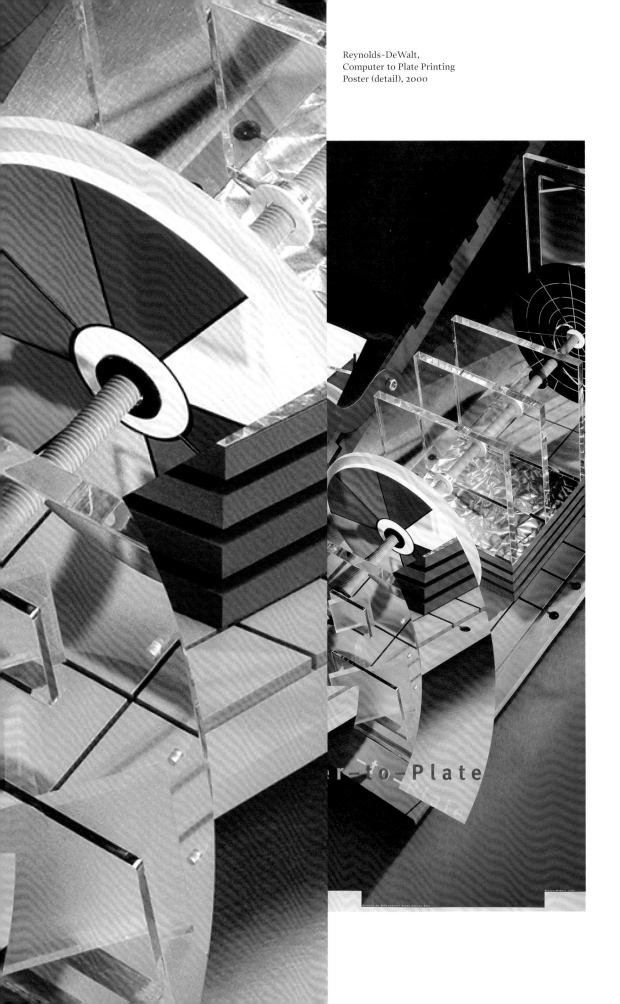

Reynolds-DeWalt,
Computer to Plate Printing
Poster (detail), 2000

A Plexiglas model was designed as an abstract representation of digital printing from computer to plate and photographed from many points of view to create the final poster image, which combines several points of view to animate the image and the printing process.

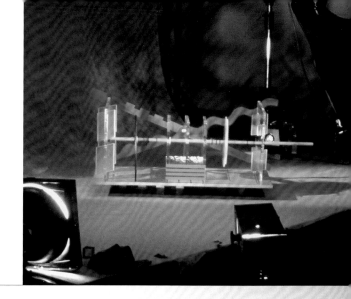

Reynolds-DeWalt,
Computer to Plate Printing
Poster, 2000, offset
lithograph, 36 × 26 in.

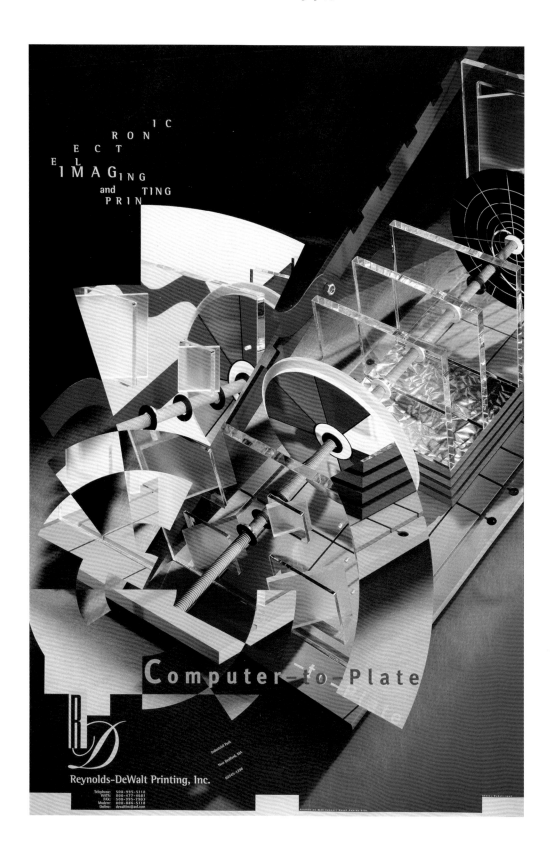

2000 Skolos-Wedell featured in *A! Diseño Ano 9 No. 53*, "Skolos-Wedell," Mexico

2001 Skolos-Wedell Home/ Studio featured in *Architectural Record*, "Residential Live/ Work"

2002 Work included in *USDesign 1975–2000*, Denver Art Museum

2002 Work included in *Vive le graphiseme!* Galerie Anatome, Paris

2003 Skolos becomes Department Head of Graphic Design at RISD

2003 Skolos becomes an AIGA Boston Fellow

2003 Skolos-Wedell Home/ Studio featured in *Boston Globe Magazine*, "Shock of the New'"

2003 Skolos-Wedell profiled in *Graphis Magazine 345*, "Skolos-Wedell in Tandem"

2003–2006 Skolos is Head of the Department of Graphic Design at RISD

2005 Skolos becomes a Full Professor at RISD

2005 Work included in *Megg's History of Graphic Design*, 4th Edition

2006 Skolos-Wedell author the book *Type, Image, Message*

2009 Work featured in *Poster Collection 17*, Lars Müller Publishers

2009 Skolos-Wedell profiled in *New Graphic* magazine, China

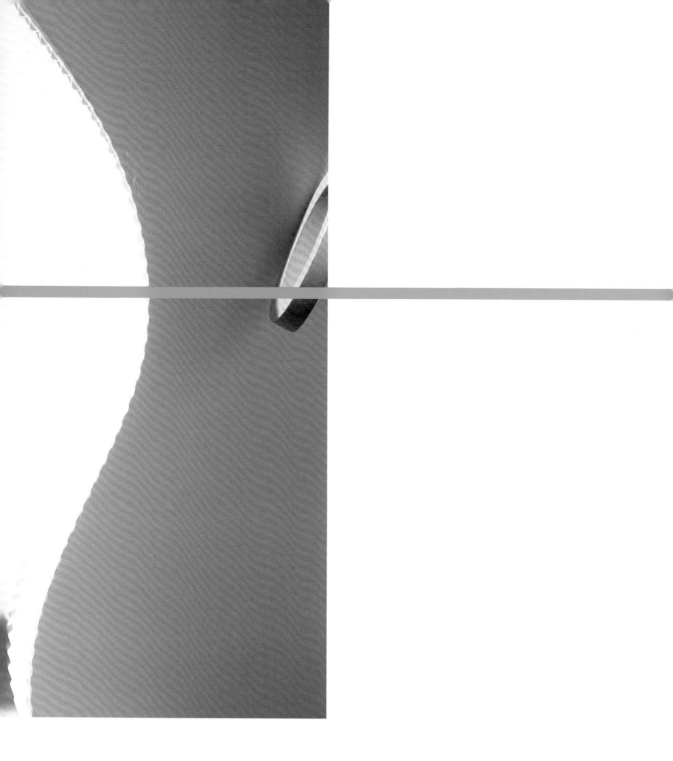

'00s: Refining a
Symbolic Language

Lyceum Fellowship Poster
(detail), 2001

Lyceum Fellowship Poster
(in process, magazine
pieces collage), 2001

The collage's large, circular,
spool-like element and
matrix of color was
inspired by the 2001
program, which called for a
textile factory design.

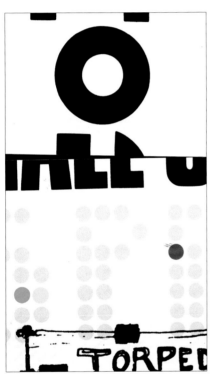

Process: collage sketch

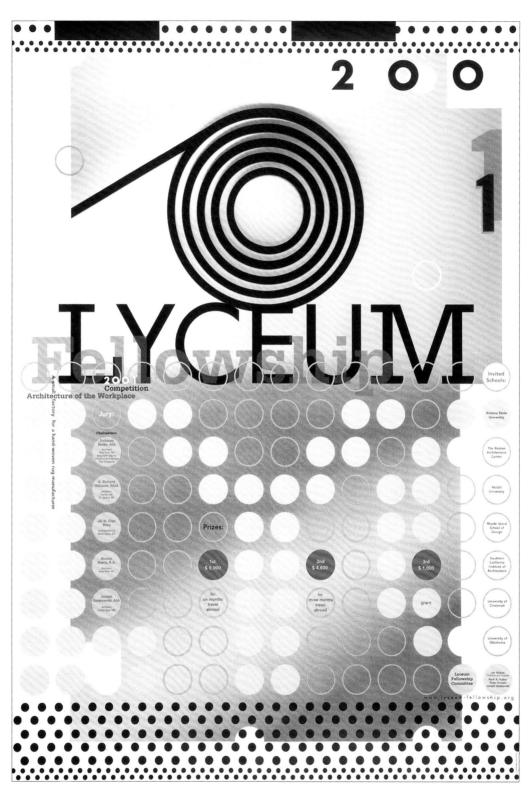

Lyceum Fellowship, Student
Architecture Competition
Poster, 2001, silk screen,
39 ½ × 27 ½ in.

Rhode Island School of Design, Faculty Biennial Exhibition Poster (in process, collages), 2001

Left: A collage evoking a museum entryway and banner provided an idea for a framing device. Right: A collage's large, energetic letterforms inspired the placement of the letters "RISD."

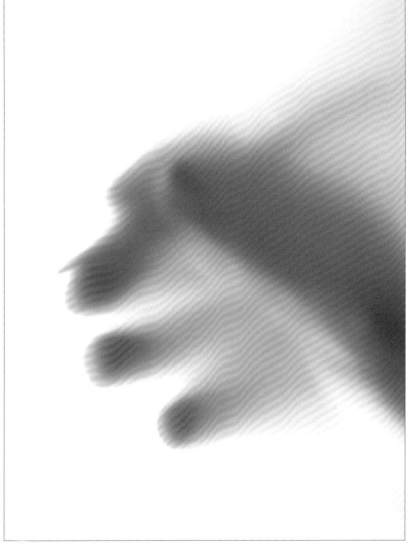

The primary image was of a hand holding a pencil, pressed against a sheet of translucent rubber to create the effect of an artist touching the poster's picture plane.

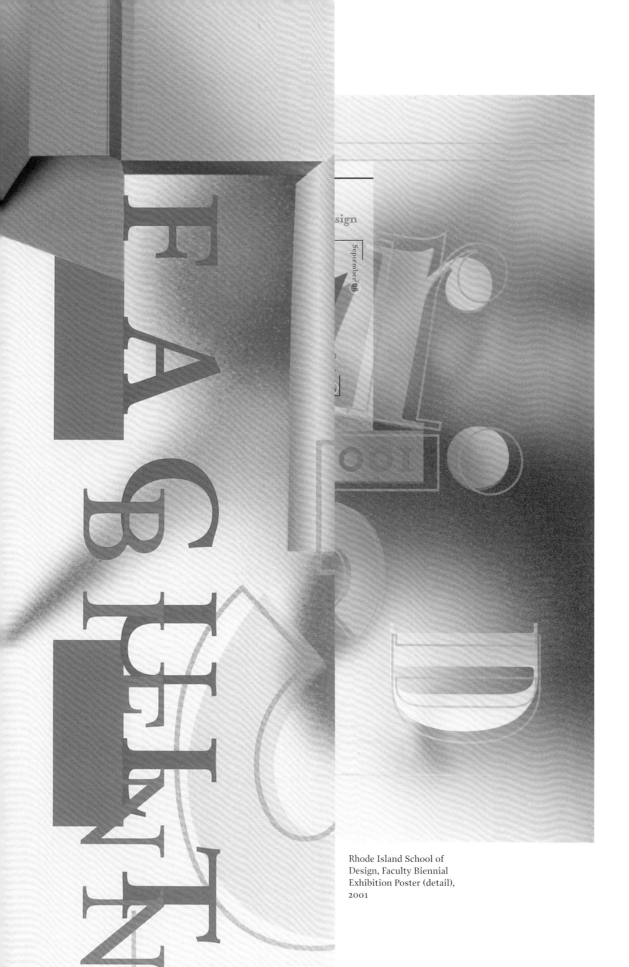

Rhode Island School of
Design, Faculty Biennial
Exhibition Poster (detail),
2001

The collage-inspired entryway
element was constructed
from Bristol board and
photographed and combined
with the photograph of the
hand in Photoshop.

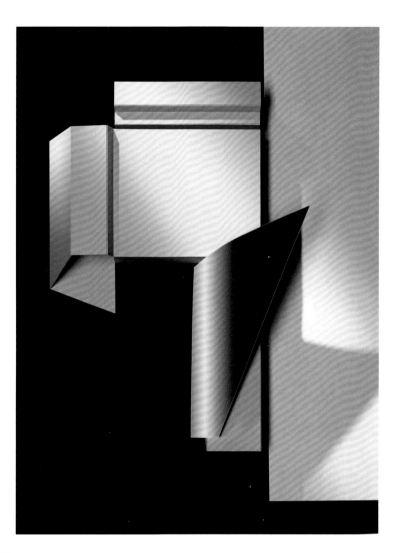

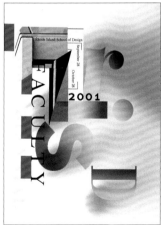

Rhode Island School of
Design, Faculty Biennial
Exhibition Poster (in
process, sketch harmonizing
the photographic idea, the
collage ideas, and the poster
content), 2001

Rhode Island School of
Design, Faculty Biennial
Exhibition Poster, 2001, silk
screen, 50 ½ × 35 ½ in.

Opposite: Lyceum Fellowship Poster (in process, landscape photograph and one of many digital mock-ups), 2002

Lyceum Fellowship, Student Architecture Competition Poster, 2002, silk screen, 50 ½ × 35 ½ in.

The 2002 program called for the design of a nature observatory that amplified ways that architecture frames landscape.

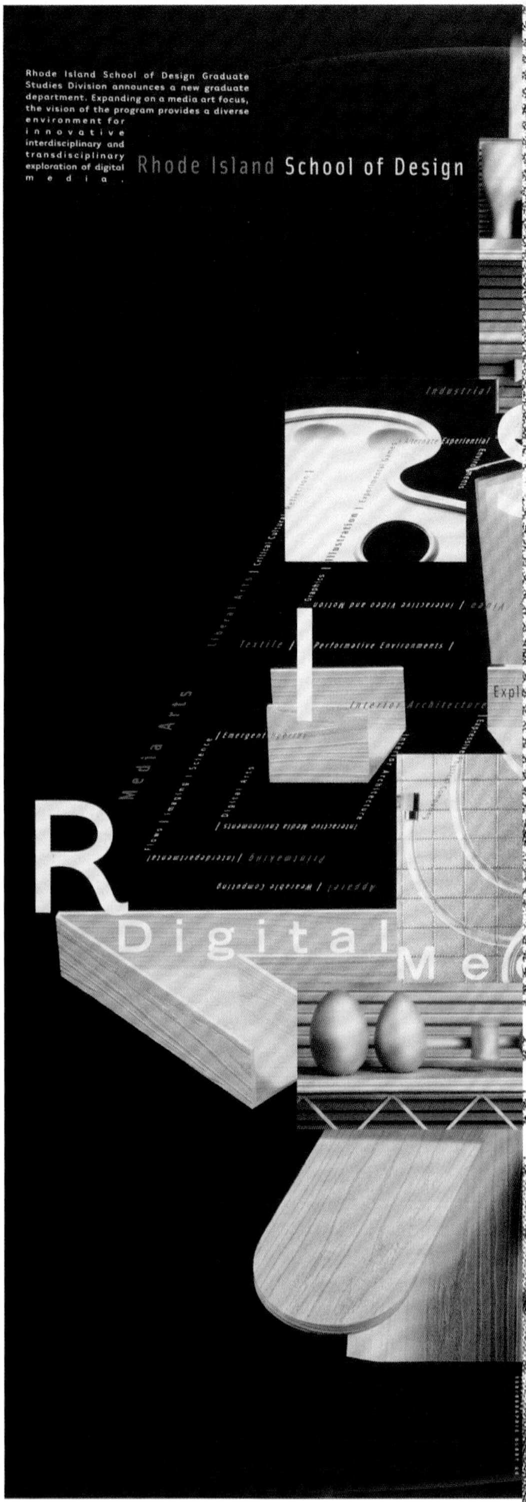

Opposite: RISD Digital
Media MFA Poster (in
process, model constructed
of foam core and covered
with wood grain paper and
floating white panels
to house a collection of
inset images representing
various types of art media
and practice), 2002

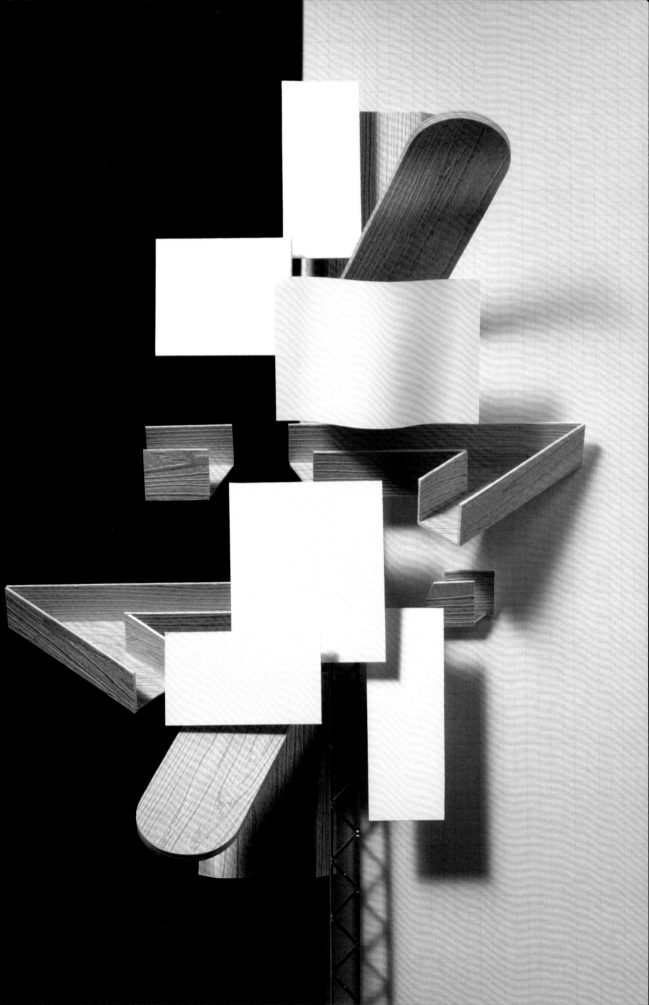

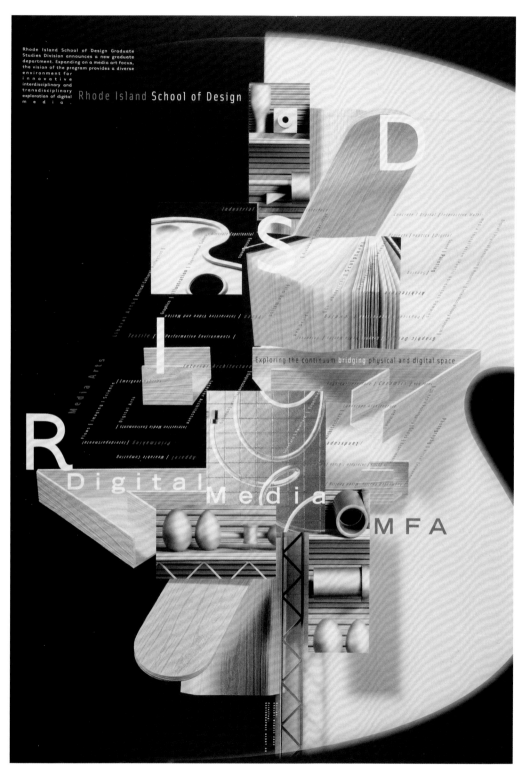

RISD Digital Media MFA
Poster, 2002, silk screen,
50 ½ × 35 ½ in.

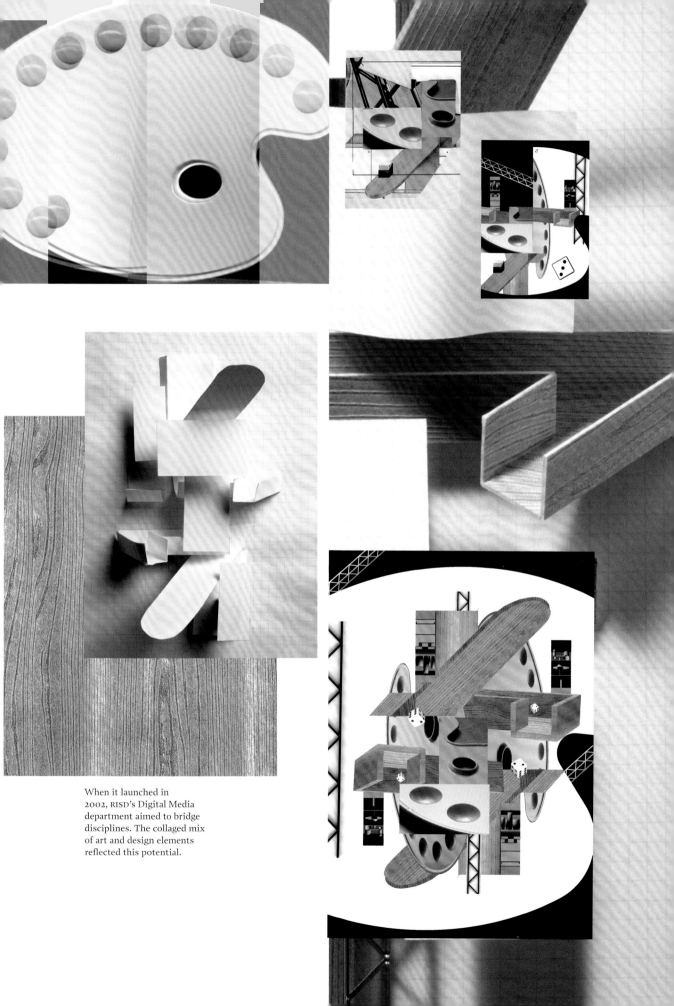

When it launched in
2002, RISD's Digital Media
department aimed to bridge
disciplines. The collaged mix
of art and design elements
reflected this potential.

Below: The box-like elements in this magazine collage formed the underpinnings for the 2003 Lyceum Fellowship program, "Reinventing the House on Wheels," which asked architecture students to propose innovative approaches to prefabricated mobile homes.

Model construction was made of velvet paper-covered foam core and metallic painted plastic elements, approx. 30 × 30 in.

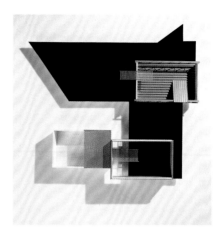

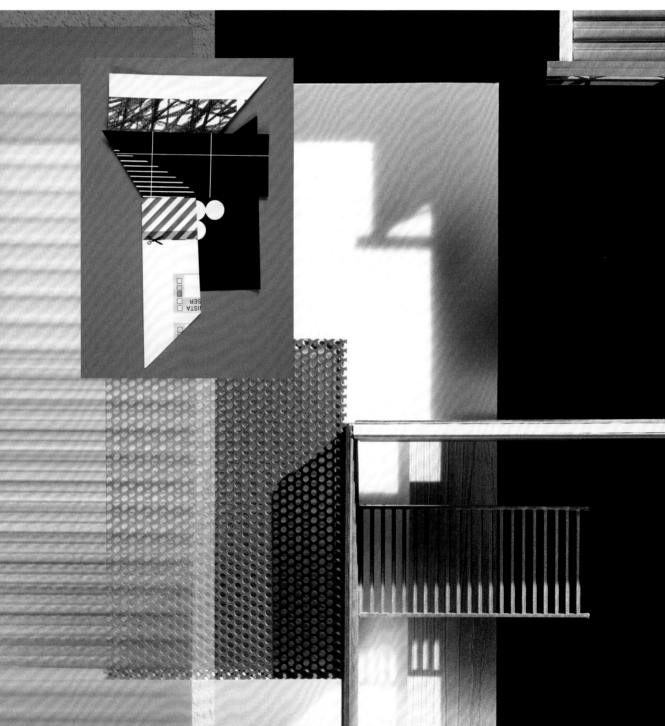

Lyceum Fellowship, Student
Architecture Competition
Poster, 2003, silk screen,
50 ½ × 35 ½ in.

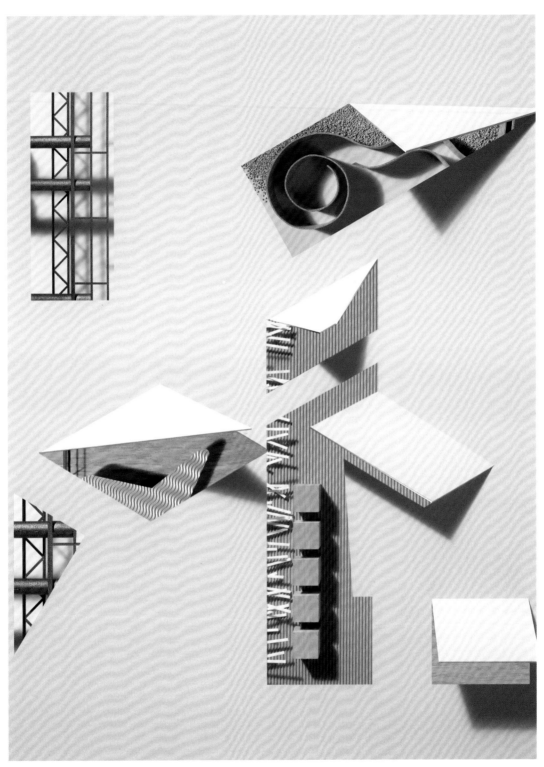

Lyceum Fellowship, Student Architecture Competition Poster (in process, primary photograph of flat surface with openings, housed individual photographs composed of various landscape-oriented surfaces), 2004

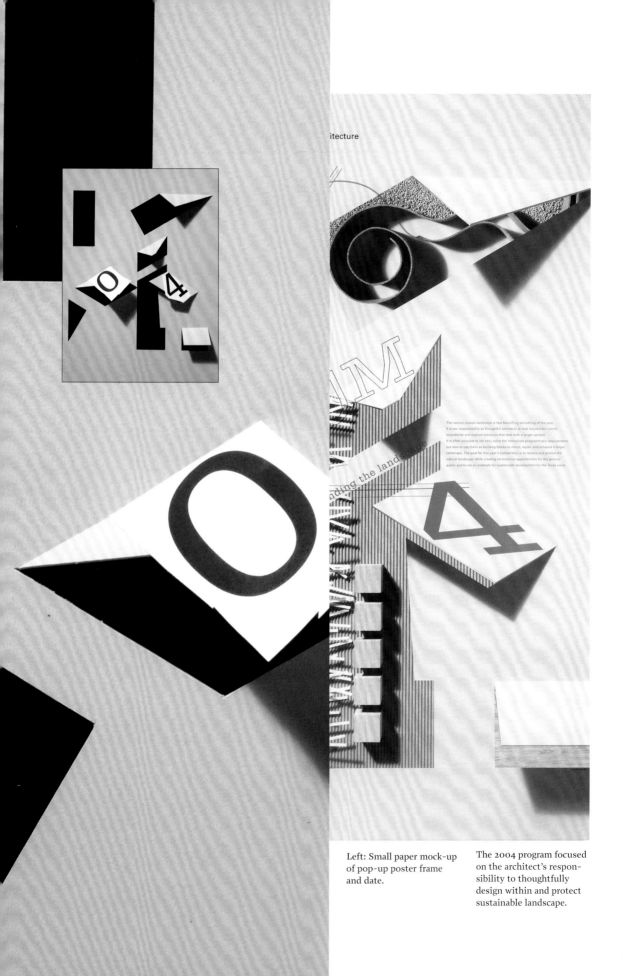

The natural coastal landscape is fast becoming something of the past. It is our responsibility as thoughtful architects to look beyond our clients' boundaries and explore solutions that deal with a larger context. It is often possible to not only solve the immediate programmatic requirements but also to use them as building blocks to mend, repair, and enhance a larger landscape. The goal for this year's competition is to restore and protect the natural landscape while creating recreational opportunities for the general public and to set an example for sustainable development for the Texas coast.

Left: Small paper mock-up of pop-up poster frame and date.

The 2004 program focused on the architect's responsibility to thoughtfully design within and protect sustainable landscape.

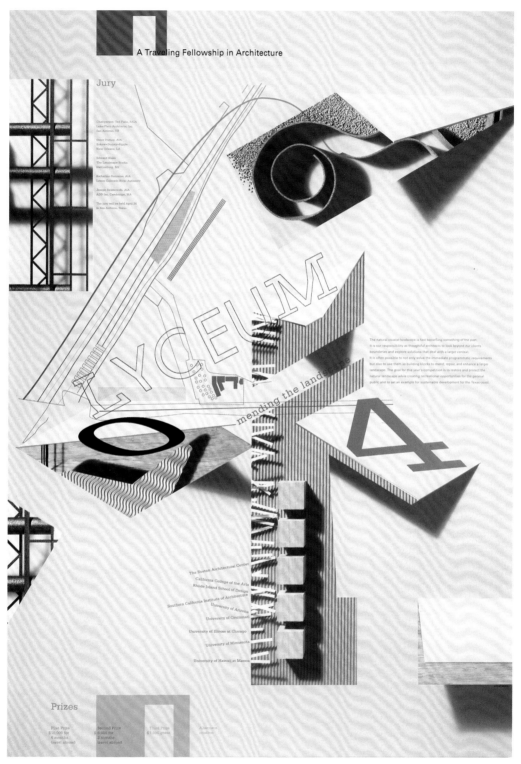

Opposite: Lyceum
Fellowship Poster (detail),
2004

Lyceum Fellowship, Student
Architecture Competition
Poster, 2004, silk screen,
50 ½ × 35 ½ in.

For the Lyceum Fellowship, Student Architecture Competition Poster, 2005 structural elements were folded around photographs of a human figure (Nancy) to illustrate the 2005 program theme, "wearable architecture."

traveling

5

fellowship

Jury:

competition

architecture

Prizes:

First prize:
$10,000 for 6 months
travel abroad

Second prize:
$6,000 for 3 months
travel abroad

Third prize:
$1,000 grant

Alternate:
Citation

Lyceum Fellowship, Student
Architecture Competition
Poster, 2005, silk screen,
50 ½ × 35 ½ in.

Light of Hope for Indonesia
Poster, 2005, silk screen,
50 ½ × 35 ½ in.

'00s

156

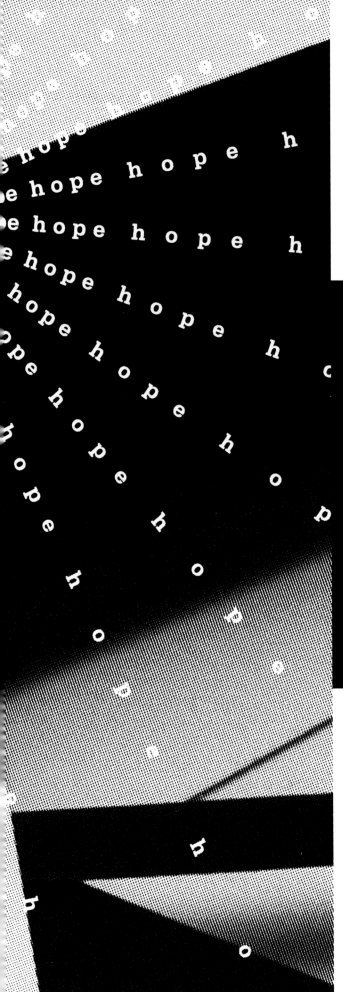

Poster was part of an invitational international collection exhibited in Jakarta, Yogyakarta, Bandung, and Surabaya from 2005—2006 to honor the loss and strengthen hope after the December 2004 Indian Ocean earthquake and tsunami.

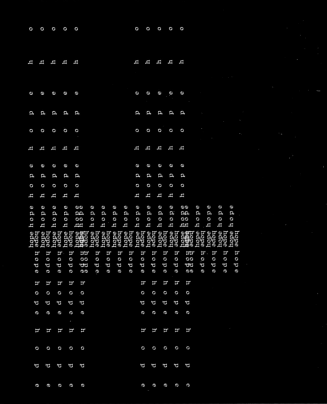

Light of Hope for Indonesia
Poster (details), 2005

Hidden infrastructural systems informed the design of the photographic model (below), constructed of foam core and covered in various papers for the Lyceum Fellowship, Student Architecture Competition, 2006.

The 2006 program called for the design of a penthouse on top of a mixed-use industrial building during Boston's "big dig."

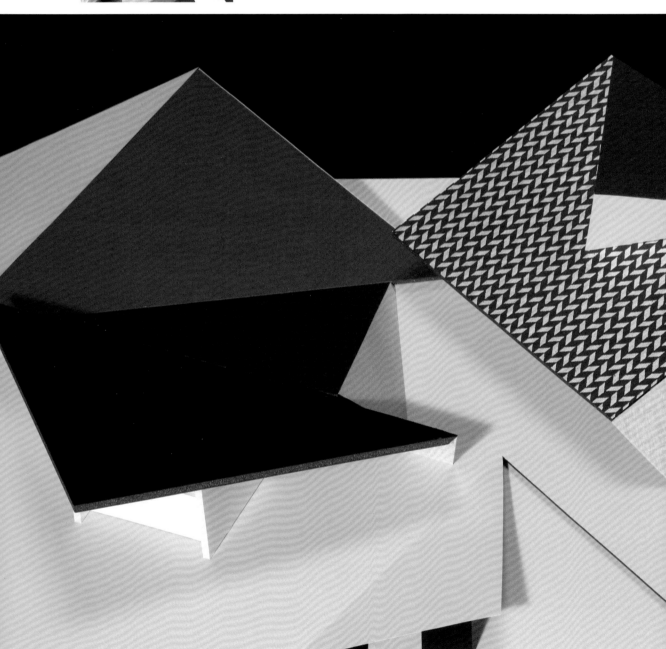

Lyceum Fellowship,
Student Architecture
Competition Poster
(detail), 2006

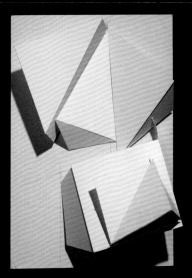

Lyceum Fellowship, Student
Architecture Competition
Poster (in process, preliminary
paper construction and
collage mock-ups), 2006

Left: Book press was shot
separately and assembled
into the final poster image
to heighten the image's
industrial, mechanical quality.

Lyceum Fellowship, Student
Architecture Competition
Poster, 2006, silk screen,
50 ½ × 35 ½ in.

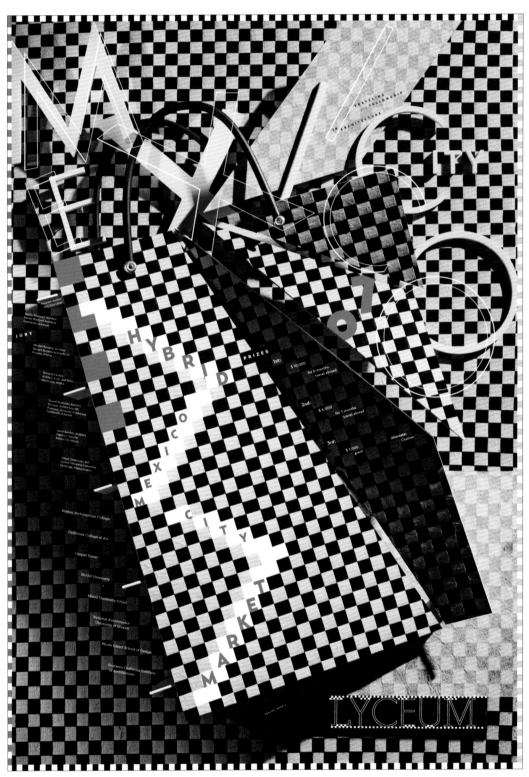

Lyceum Fellowship, Student
Architecture Competition
Poster, 2007, silk screen,
50 ½ × 35 ½ in.

The 2007 program called
for the design of a marketplace in Mexico City.

Opposite: Lyceum
Fellowship Poster (in
process, foam core model
detail and collage sketches
imagining a shopping bag
as a container), 2007

Opposite: Lyceum
Fellowship, Student
Architecture Competition
Poster (in process, photo
shoot), 2008

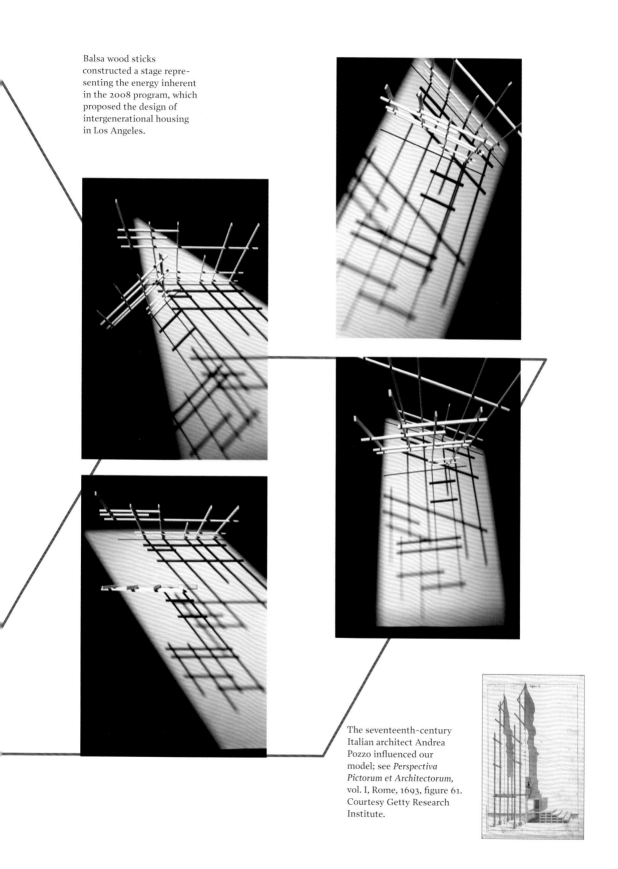

Balsa wood sticks
constructed a stage representing the energy inherent
in the 2008 program, which
proposed the design of
intergenerational housing
in Los Angeles.

The seventeenth-century
Italian architect Andrea
Pozzo influenced our
model; see *Perspectiva
Pictorum et Architectorum,*
vol. I, Rome, 1693, figure 61.
Courtesy Getty Research
Institute.

Lyceum Fellowship, Student
Architecture Competition
Poster, 2008, silk screen,
50 ½ × 35 ½ in.

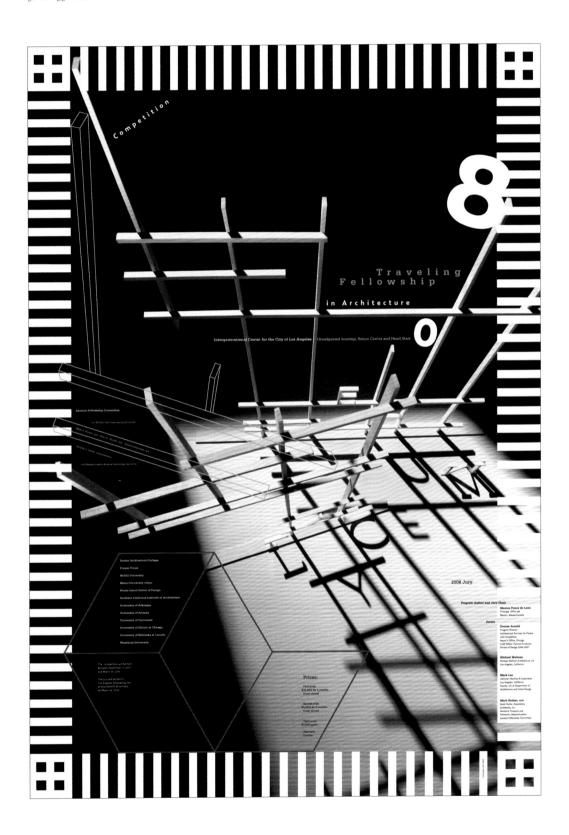

Kahlo Rivera 100 Poster
(in process, set-up for
the photo shoot with
two transparent graphic
portraits of Frida Kahlo
and Diego Rivera casting
shadows on canvas and
woodgrain surfaces), 2008

The poster was part of an
invitational exhibition
of 100 designers' posters
commemorating Frida
Kahlo and Diego Rivera.

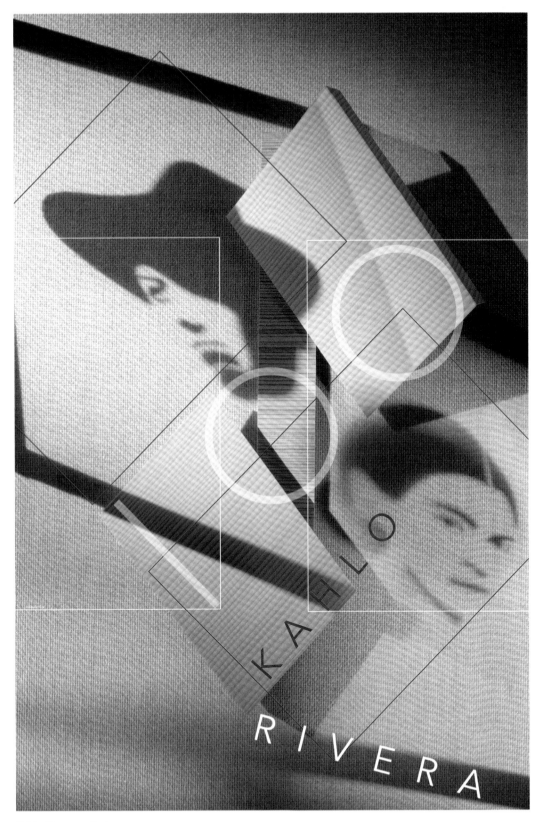

Kahlo Rivera 100 Poster,
2008, silk screen,
50 ½ × 35 ½ in.

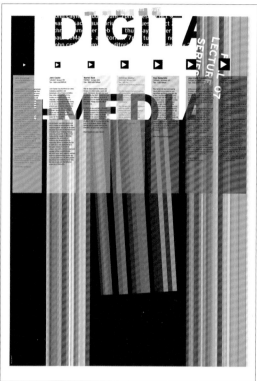

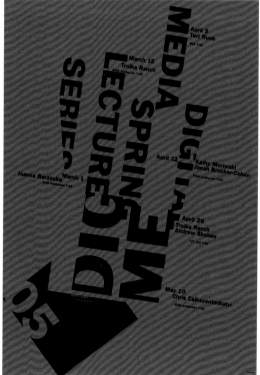

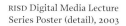
RISD Digital Media Lecture
Series Poster (detail), 2003

RISD Digital Media Lecture
Series Poster, Fall 2003,
offset lithograph, 34 × 24 in.

Opposite, clockwise from
top left: RISD Digital Media
Lecture Series Posters,
Spring 2003, Fall 2007,
Spring 2005, Spring 2004,
offset lithographs, 34 × 24 in.

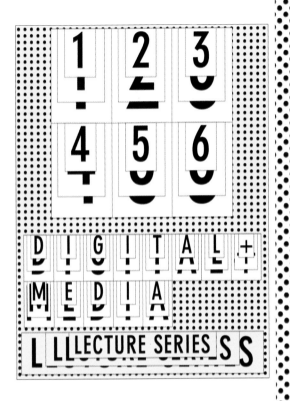

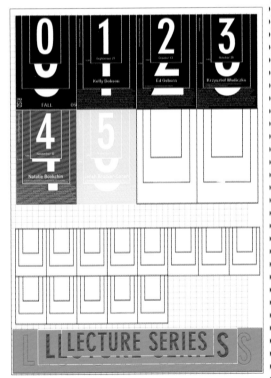

RISD Digital Media Lecture
Series Poster (in process,
preliminary sketches),
2009

RISD Digital Media Lecture
Series Poster (detail), 2009

RISD Museum/Metcalf Auditorium

4

November 10

TUES

8 PM

Natalie Bookchin

in collaboration with the Malcolm S. Forbes Center for Culture and Media
Studies and the Department of Modern Culture and Media at Brown University

Natalie Bookchin is an artist with a background in   photography a
Her recent videos and installations that address   current conditi
connectivity and the impact of everyday uses of   new technologi
see, represent, and understand ourselves and the   world around
has been exhibited at PS1, Mass MOCA, the Generali Foundation, the Walker Art Cen
Pompidou Centre, MOCA Los Angeles, the Whitney Museum, the Tate, and Creative T
received grants from Creative Capital, California Arts Council, the Guggenheim Foun
Durfee Foundation, the Rockefeller Foundation, California Community Foundation, N
Council for the Arts, Daniel Langlois Foundation, and a COLA Artist Fellowship. Book
the School of the Art Institute of Chicago, the Whitney Independent Study Program, a
Purchase. She lives and works in Los Angeles, where she is co-Director of the Photo
Program in the Art School at CalArts.

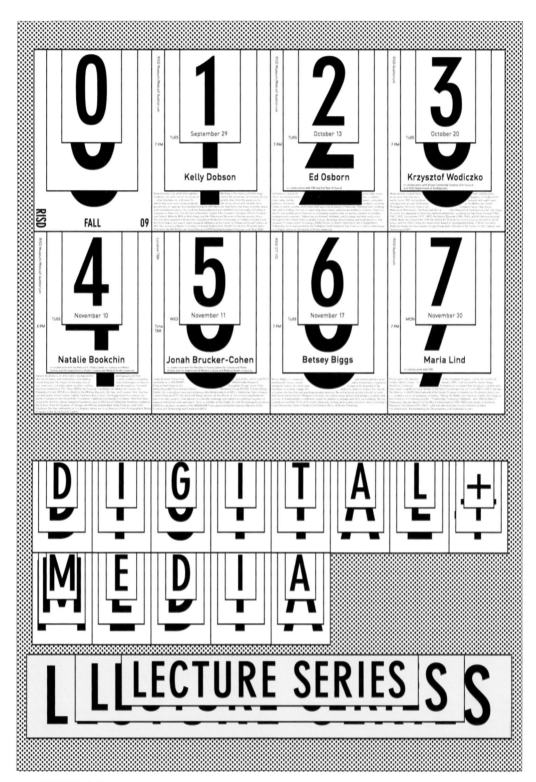

RISD Digital Media Lecture
Series Poster, 2009, Fuji
OnSet S-20 print,
50 ½ × 35 ½ in.

Lyceum Fellowship, Student
Architecture Competition
Poster, 2009, Fuji OnSet
S-20 print, 50 ½ × 35 ½ in.

Opposite: Poster iterations
and model detail. The 2009
program called for the design
of a metalsmithing studio
at Penland School of Crafts,
which informed the red-hot
tone of the photograph.

Unesco, Languages Matter!
photograph (detail), 2009

Enigmatic letter-like
structures were arranged
to express the feeling of
speech without referencing
a specific language system.

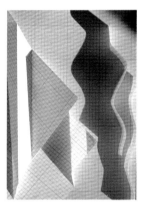

Unesco, Languages Matter!
Poster (in process, photograph
of miniature paper model and
testing of typographic
elements), 2009

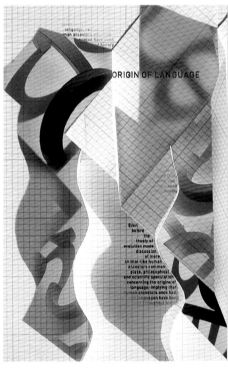

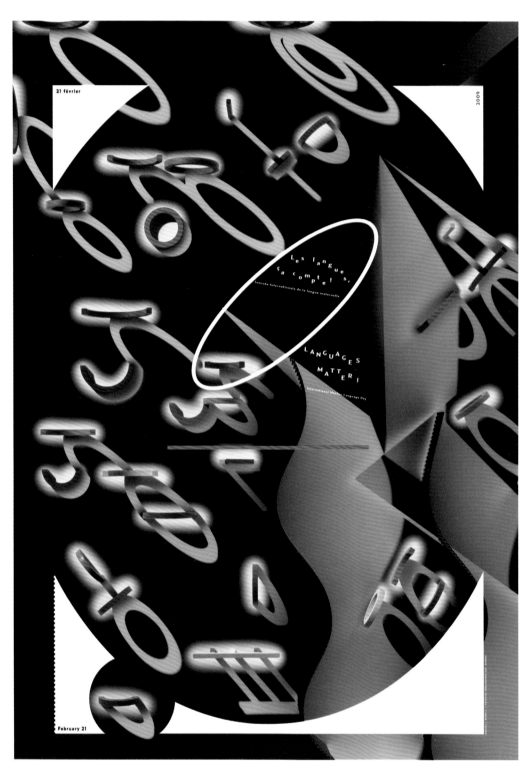

Unesco, Languages Matter!
Poster, 2009, celebrating
International Mother
Language Day, Fuji OnSet S-20
print, 50 ½ × 35 ½ in.

2010 Chopin poster wins a Gold Medal in the *International Poster Biennial*, Warsaw

2010 Studio featured in *2+3d Design* magazine, "Doswiadczanie Przestrzeni," Poland

2011 Chopin poster wins a Silver Medal in the *International Poster Biennial*, Lahti, Finland

2011 Skolos and Wedell author the book *Graphic Design Process*

2011 Studio featured in *étapes: Design et Culture Visuelle* magazine, France

2011–2013 Skolos is Head of the Department of Graphic Design at RISD

2013 Solo exhibition, Skolos-Wedell *Persona*, Galeria Sztuki Torun, Poland

2014 Delphax Fonts poster included in *Designing Modern Women 1890–1990*, Museum of Modern Art, New York

2014-17 Skolos is Dean of Architecture and Design at RISD

2017 Skolos and Wedell are awarded the Medal of the AIGA

2018 *Give and Take: Poster Design by Nancy Skolos and Tom Wedell*, San Diego State University

2018 Skolos and Wedell are Commencement Speakers at the University of Minnesota, College of Design

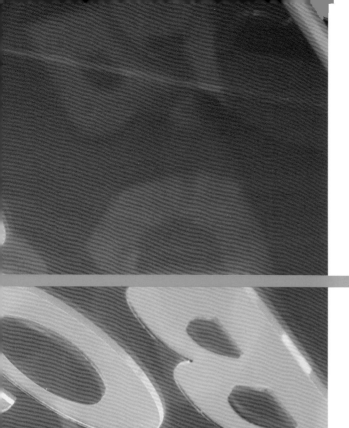

'10s: Pushing Type
and Image

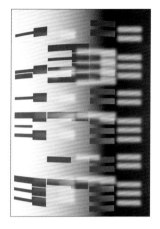
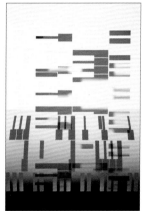

Chopin Anew Poster (in process, various lighting and curvature of the Bristol board keyboard), 2010

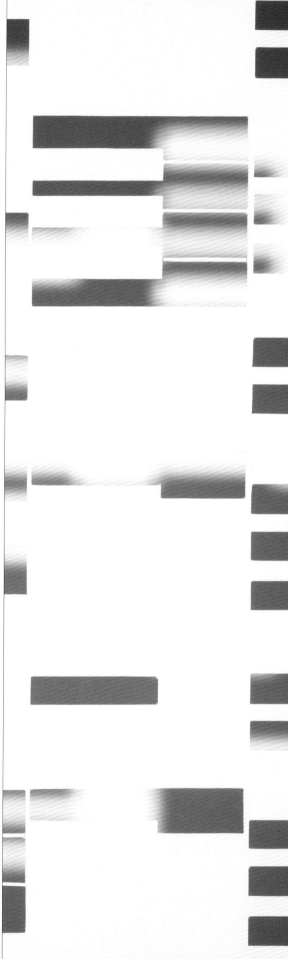

Chopin Anew Poster (in process, marrying the type forms to the keyboard)

Chopin Anew Poster, detail of keyboard cut out of Bristol board), 2010

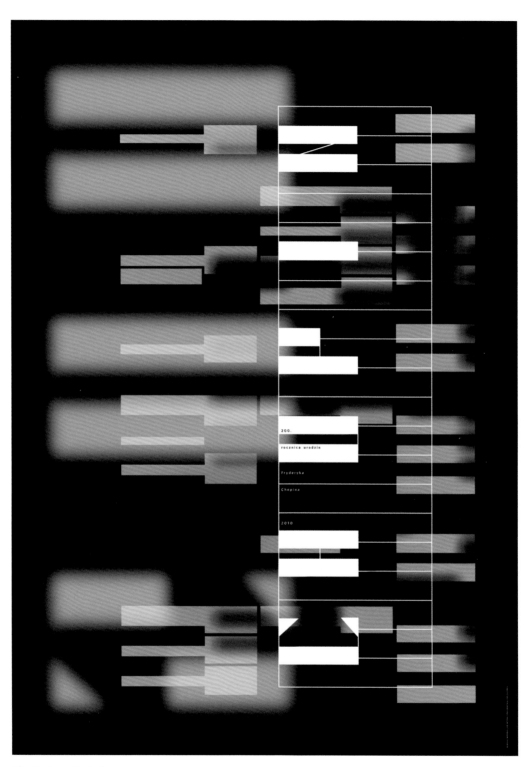

Chopin Anew Poster for
the 22nd Annual Poster
Biennial celebrating
Frederick Chopin's
200th Birthday, Warsaw,
2010, Fuji OnSet S-20 print,
50 ½ × 35 ½ in.

AIGA Boston   *honoring*
                               Matthew Carter

September 24, 2010
Cambridge Public Library

Opposite: AIGA Boston, Honoring Matthew Carter Poster, 2010, Fuji OnSet S-20 print, 50 ½ × 35 ½ in.

Below: Honoring Matthew Carter Poster (in process, assorted typefaces designed by Carter were printed and positioned with tape to determine their arrangement in camera)

The poster was part of a series of images of each letter of Carter's name, designed by Boston AIGA members. A display of magnifying glasses at the hardware store sparked the idea for the poster— to magnify the detail and precision in Matthew Carter's type designs.

Honoring Matthew Carter
Poster (detail), 2010

Honoring Matthew Carter
Poster (in process, detail of
photo set-up), 2010

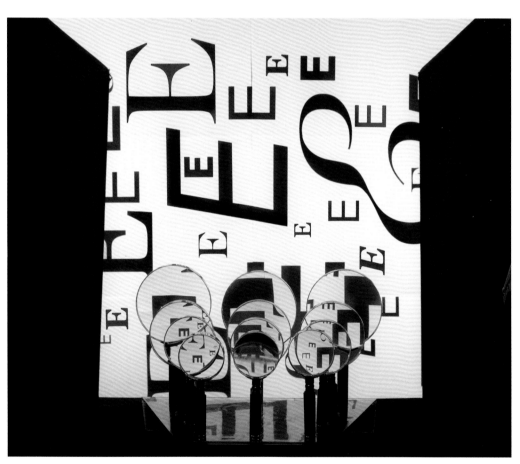

Honoring Matthew Carter
Poster (in process, photo
set-up with magnifiers
positioned in front of the
background arrangement of
Carter's letterforms), 2010

Lyceum Fellowship Poster
(in process, photo shoot),
2011

'10s

Lyceum Fellowship, Student
Architecture Competition
Poster, 2011, Fuji OnSet
S-20 print, 50 ½ × 35 ½ in.

The 2011 program called
for the design of a pavilion
and rest area situated in the
Great Salt Lake Desert.

Lyceum Fellowship Poster (in process, fabricating organically shaped "desert rocks" by pouring plaster into balloons), 2011

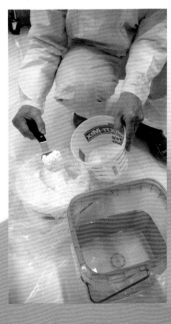

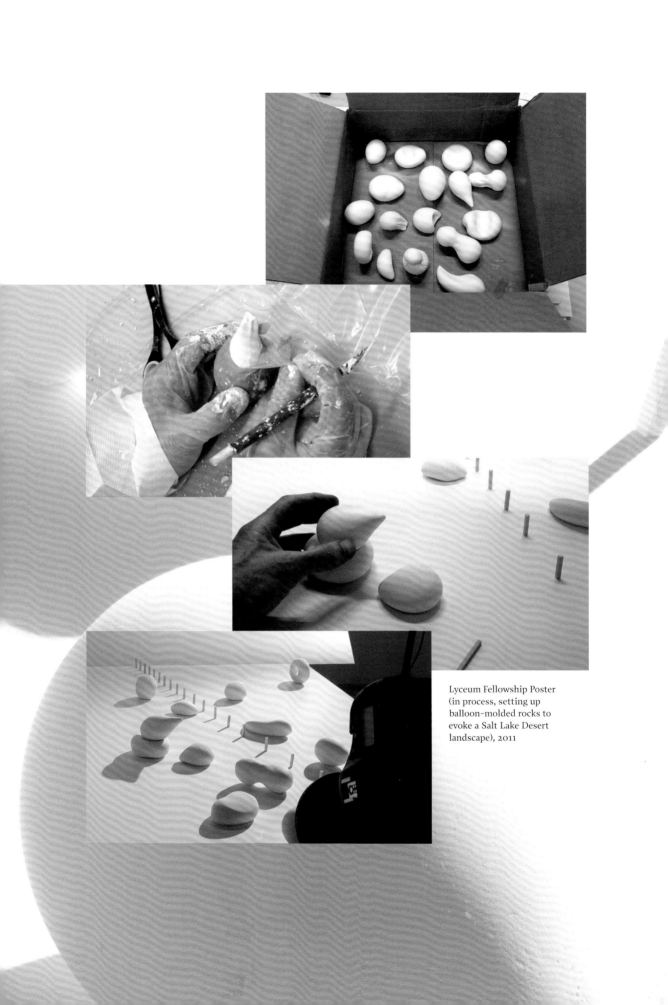

Lyceum Fellowship Poster
(in process, setting up
balloon-molded rocks to
evoke a Salt Lake Desert
landscape), 2011

Max Bruch, Eight Pieces
Poster (in process, photographic experiments), 2011

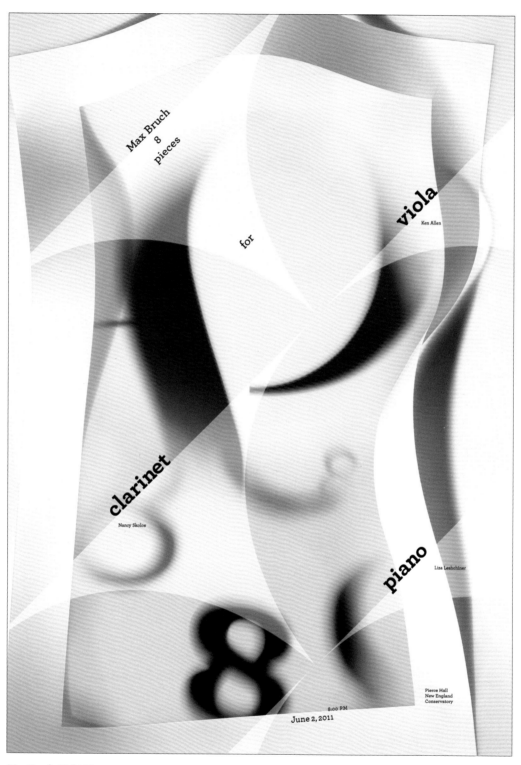

Max Bruch, Eight Pieces
Poster, 2011, Fuji OnSet
S-20 print, 50 ½ × 35 ½ in.

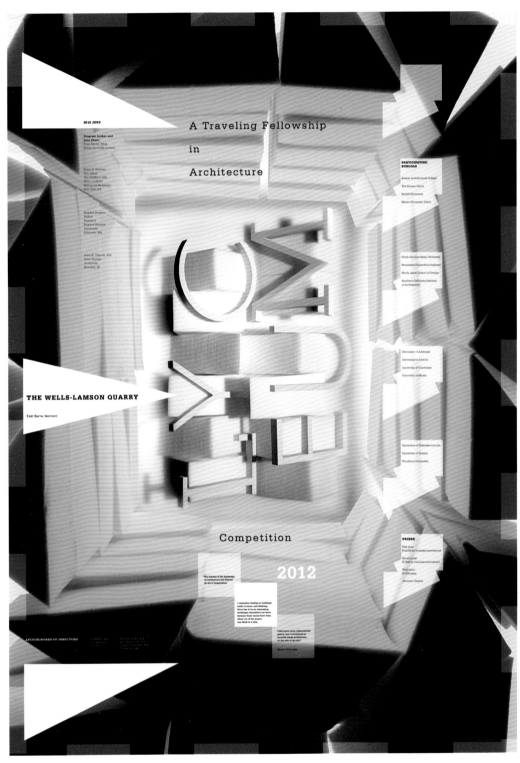

Lyceum Fellowship, Student
Architecture Competition
Poster, 2012, Fuji OnSet
S-20 print, 50 ½ × 35 ½ in.

The 2012 program was
sited at Wells-Lamson
Quarry, Vermont.

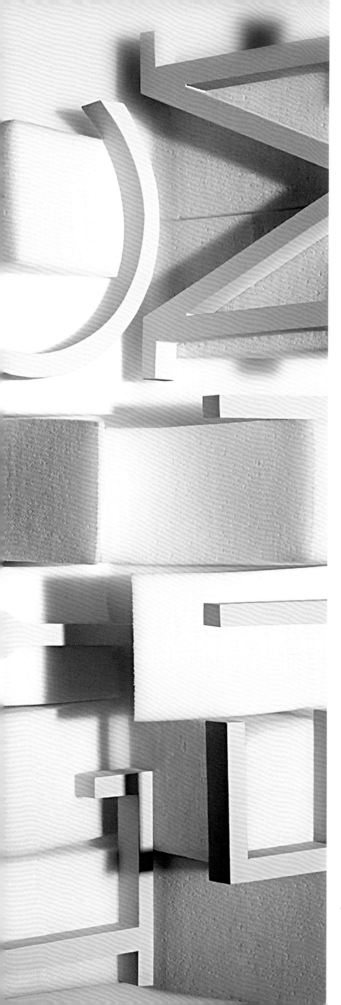

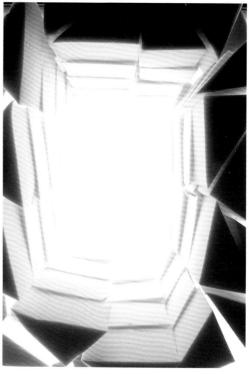

Lyceum Fellowship Poster (detail, three-dimensional "Lyceum" letters arranged with foam pieces and photo set-up of miniature stone quarry built with stacked latex make-up sponges), 2012

To Be Human Poster,
Aarhus International Poster
Show (AIPS), Dansk Plakat
Museum, 2012, Fuji OnSet
S-20 print, 50 ½ × 35 ½ in.

To Be Human Poster
(in process, early sketch of a
triptych configuration), 2012

to be human

Public Bike Poster (in process, multiple bike details edited and reconfigured to match the gesture and structure of a collage composition), 2012

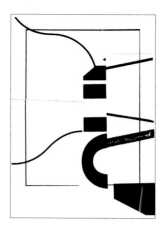
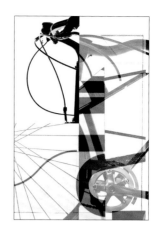

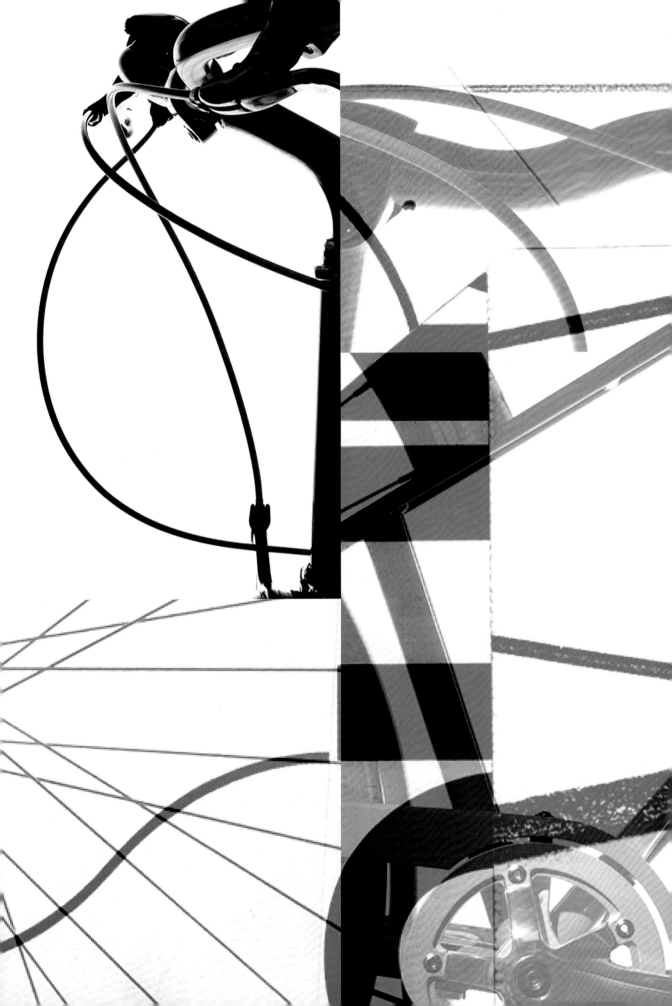

Public Bike Poster, Public
Works poster series,
commissioned by Public
Bike, 2012, Fuji OnSet S-20
print, 50 ½ × 35 ½ in.

The 2013 program challenged students to construct an architecture project addressing a problem in their community.

Lyceum Fellowship Poster (in process, map-like folding paper structure representing the construction of an architectural program), 2013

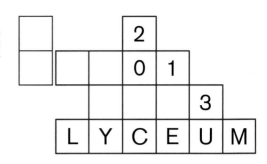

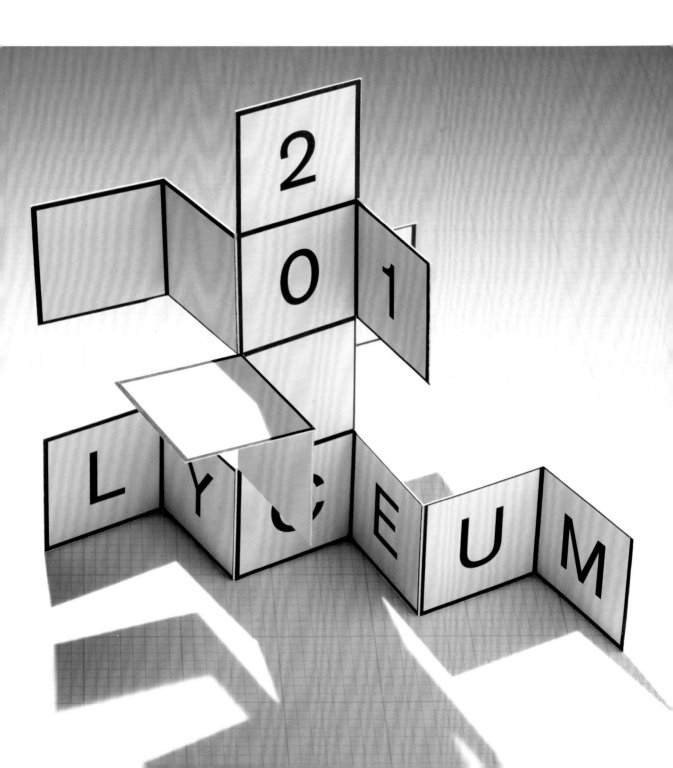

Lyceum Fellowship, Student
Architecture Competition
Poster, 2013, Fuji OnSet
S-20 print, 50 ½ × 35 ½ in.

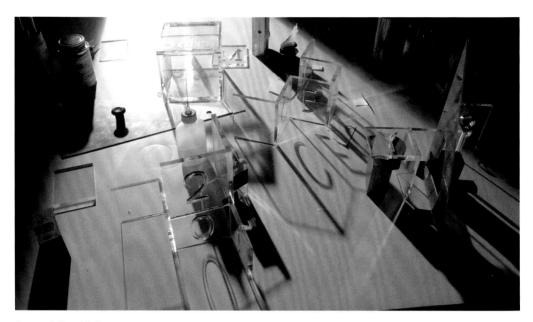

Lyceum Fellowship Poster
(in process, lasercut
Plexiglas model assembly
based on folded paper
mock-up), 2013

Skolos-Wedell *Persona*
Exhibition Poster (in
process, photograph of
Plexiglas model), 2013

Skolos, Wedell + Raynor
Poster (detail), 1982

The 2013 Skolos-Wedell *Persona* Exhibition Poster replicated the colored paper structure from the studio's 1982 poster (opposite), replacing it with clear Plexiglas to make an ethereal reference to the studio's history.

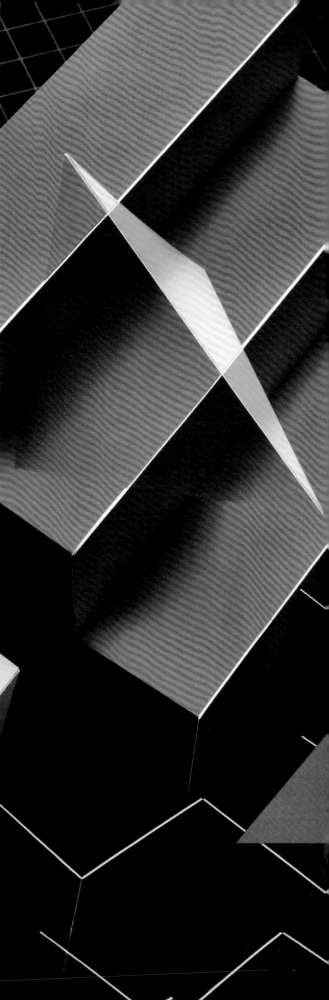

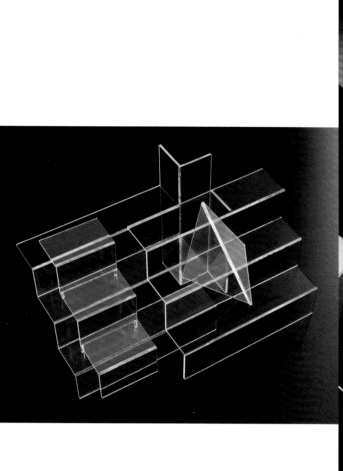

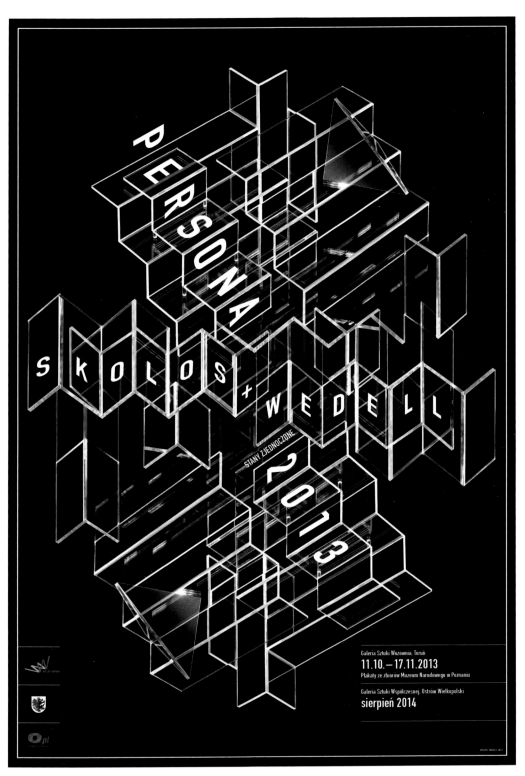

Skolos-Wedell *Persona*
Exhibition Poster, Galeria
Sztuki Wozownia, Torun,
Poland, 2013, Fuji OnSet
S-20 print, 35 ½ × 50 ½ in.

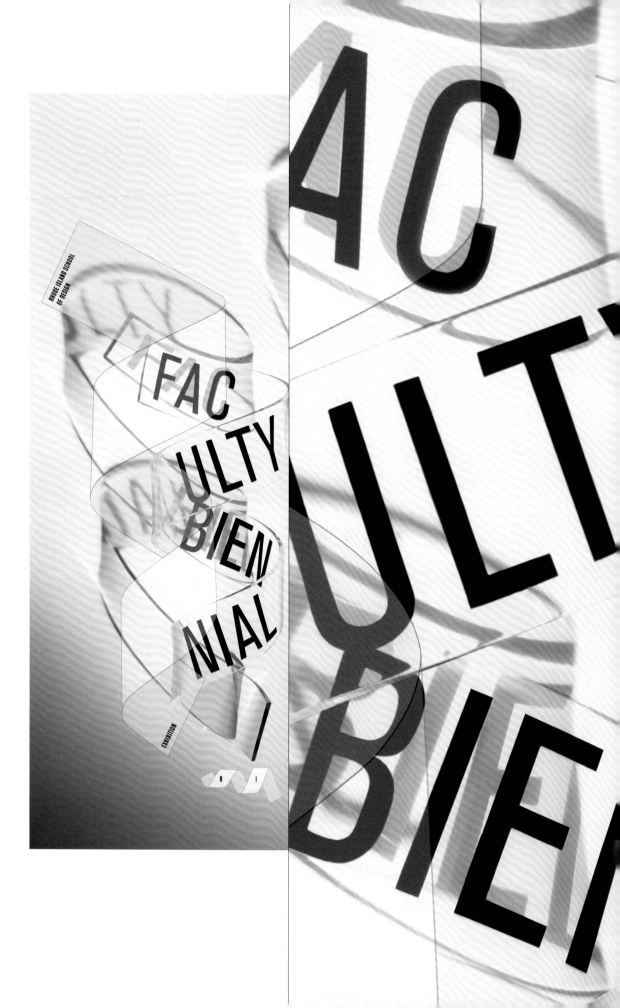

RHODE ISLAND SCHOOL OF DESIGN

FAC
ULTY
BIEN
NIAL
/

EXHIBITION

Opposite: Faculty Biennial Exhibition Poster, Rhode Island School of Design (detail), 2013

Faculty Biennial Exhibition Poster, Rhode Island School of Design (in process, paper mock-up and graphic sketch), 2013

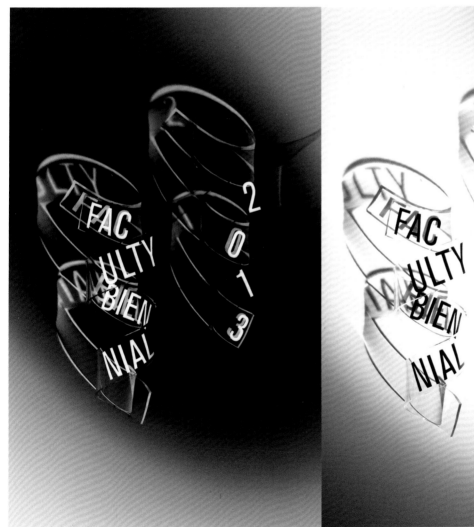

Faculty Biennial Exhibition Poster, Rhode Island School of Design (in process, transparent "ribbons" made by heating Plexiglas strips in the oven and winding them around conical forms, with vinyl letters applied directly to the Plexiglas), 2013

Faculty Biennial Exhibition
Poster, Rhode Island School
of Design, 2013, Fuji OnSet
S-20 print, 50 ½ × 35 ½ in.

Boston Book Festival
Poster (detail), 2013

5th
Annual

BOS
BOOK
BOS TOK
FESTIVAL

Oct.
2013
17–19

COPLEY SQUARE

Opposite: Boston Book
Festival Poster (in
process, sketches, paper
models, and laser-cut
model pieces), 2013

Boston Book Festival
Poster, 2013, Fuji OnSet
S-20 print, 50 ½ × 35 ½ in.

Hal Abelson Poster,
Presidential Speaker Poster
Series, Rhode Island School
of Design (detail), 2013

Hal Abelson Poster (in process,
selected sketches), 2013

Hal Abelson Poster (in process,
selected sketches), 2013

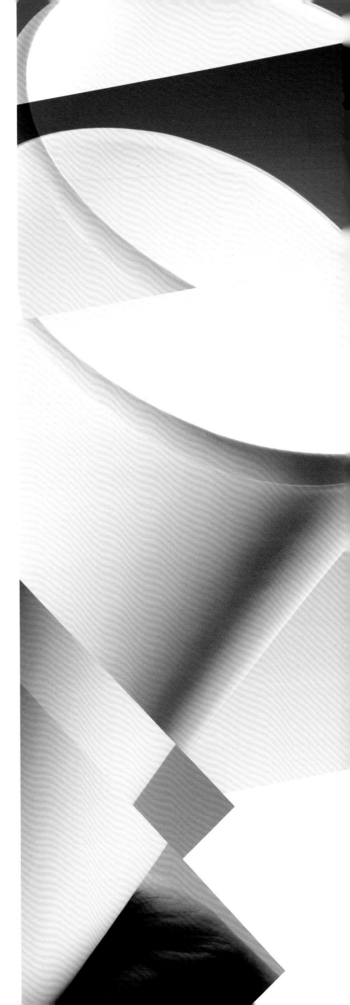

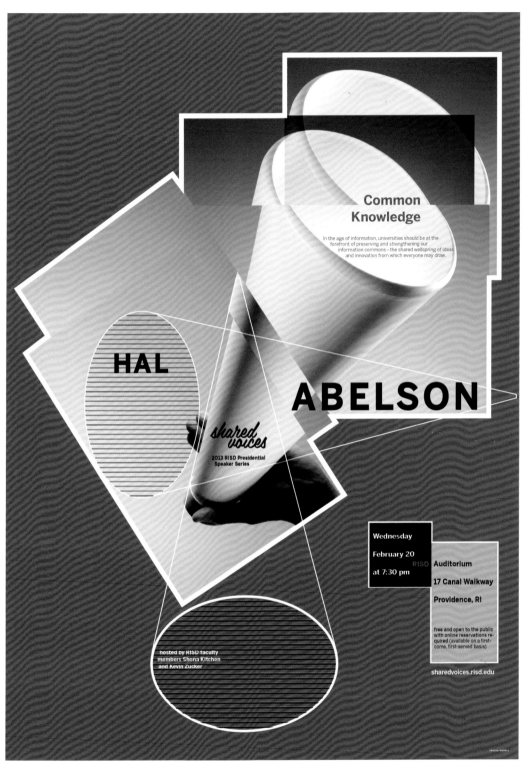

Hal Abelson Poster,
Presidential Speaker Poster
Series, Rhode Island School
of Design, 2013, offset
lithograph, 24 × 18 in.

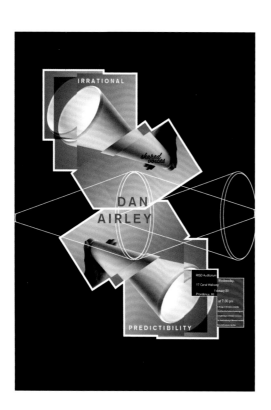

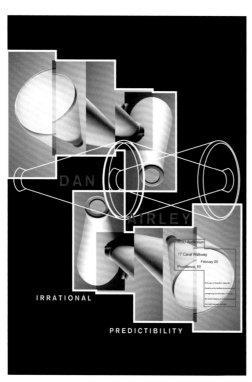

Dan Ariely Poster
(in process, selected
sketches), 2013

Dan Ariely Poster (detail),
2013

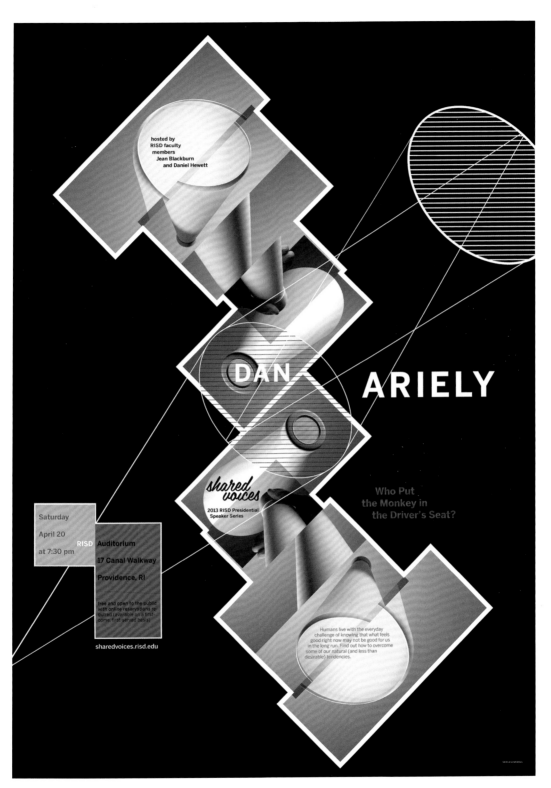

Dan Ariely Poster,
Presidential Speaker Poster
Series, Rhode Island School
of Design, 2013, offset
lithograph, 24 × 18 in.

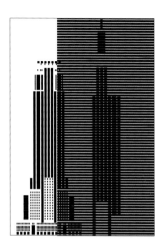

Lyceum Fellowship Poster (in process, high-contrast graphic translation of the Empire State Building, folded to make the model set whose perspective was progressively exaggerated and tested in-camera), 2015

The 2015 program asked students to reconfigure the Empire State Building into a senior living center.

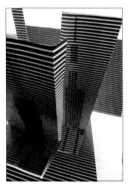

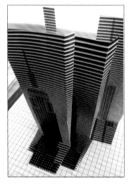

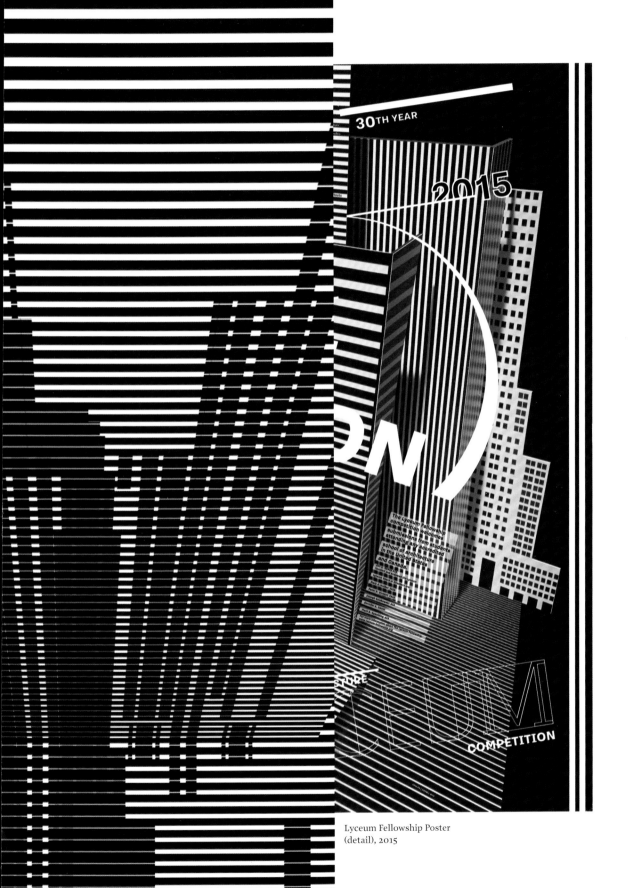

Lyceum Fellowship Poster
(detail), 2015

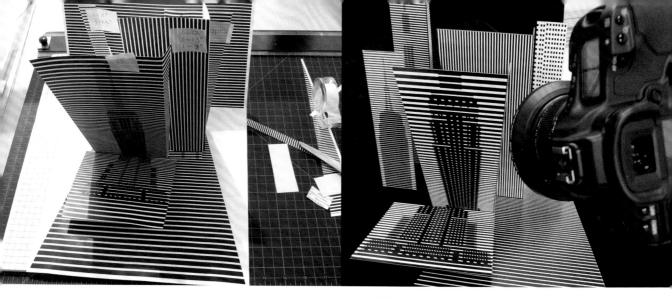

Lyceum Fellowship
Poster (in process, final
photographic model with
building images mounted
to illustration board), 2015

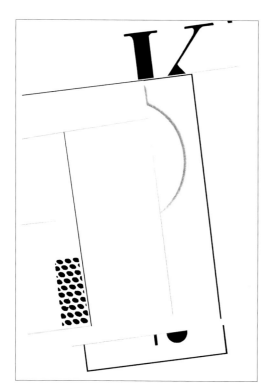

Lyceum Fellowship Poster
(in process, collage sketch
overlaid onto photograph
to generate a grid for type
placement), 2015

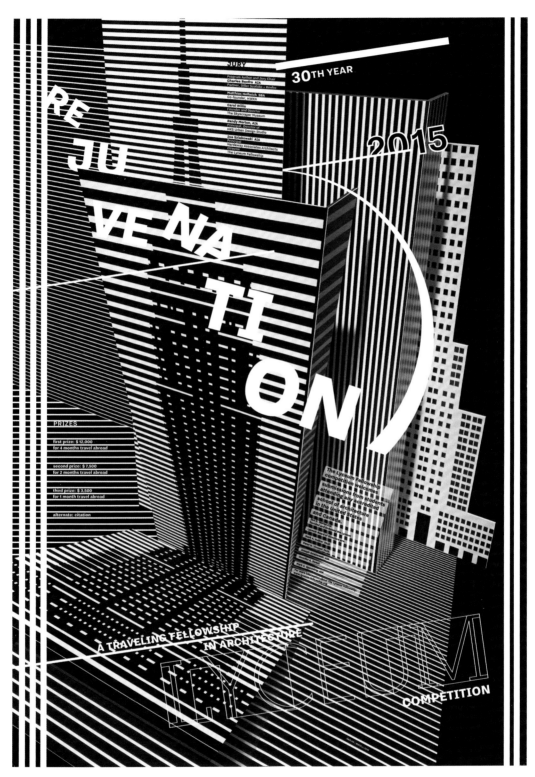

Lyceum Fellowship, Student
Architecture Competition
Poster, 2015, Fuji OnSet
S-20 print, 50 ½ × 35 ½ in.

Coexistence Poster, Special
Project for the Alliance
Graphique Internationale
(AGI) Conference (detail,
final photograph), 2015

Coexistence Poster, Special
Project for the Alliance
Graphique Internationale
(AGI) Conference (in process,
various image and type
scenarios), 2015

Coexistence Poster, Special
Project for the Alliance
Graphique Internationale
(AGI) Conference, 2015,
Fuji OnSet S-20 print,
50 ½ × 35 ½ in.

Lyceum Fellowship Poster
(detail), 2016

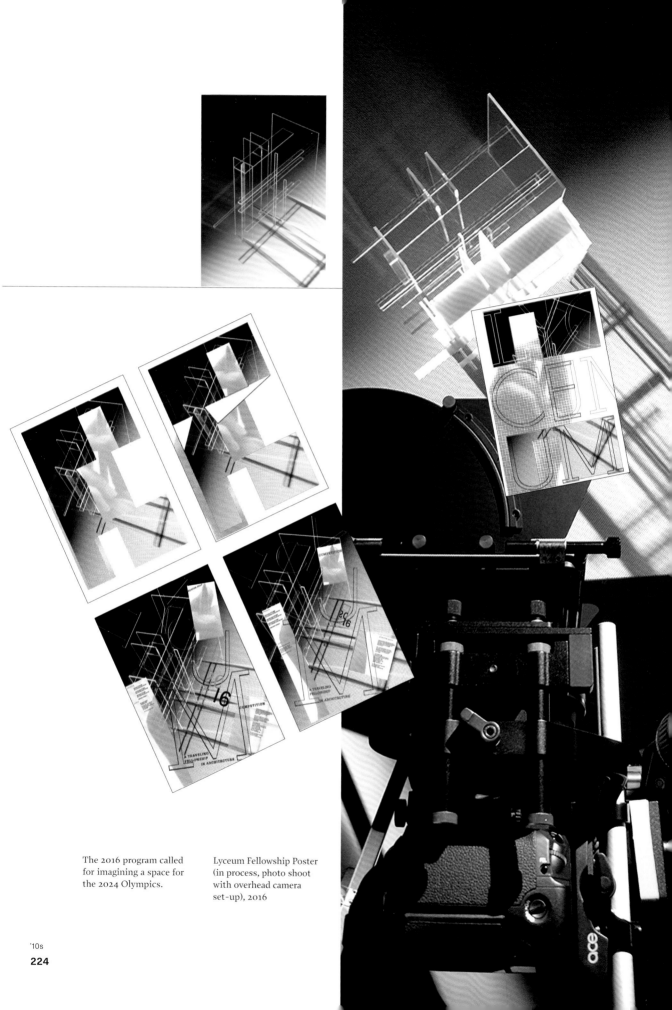

The 2016 program called for imagining a space for the 2024 Olympics.

Lyceum Fellowship Poster (in process, photo shoot with overhead camera set-up), 2016

Lyceum Fellowship, Student
Architecture Competition
Poster, 2016, Fuji OnSet
S-20 print, 50 ½ × 35 ½ in.

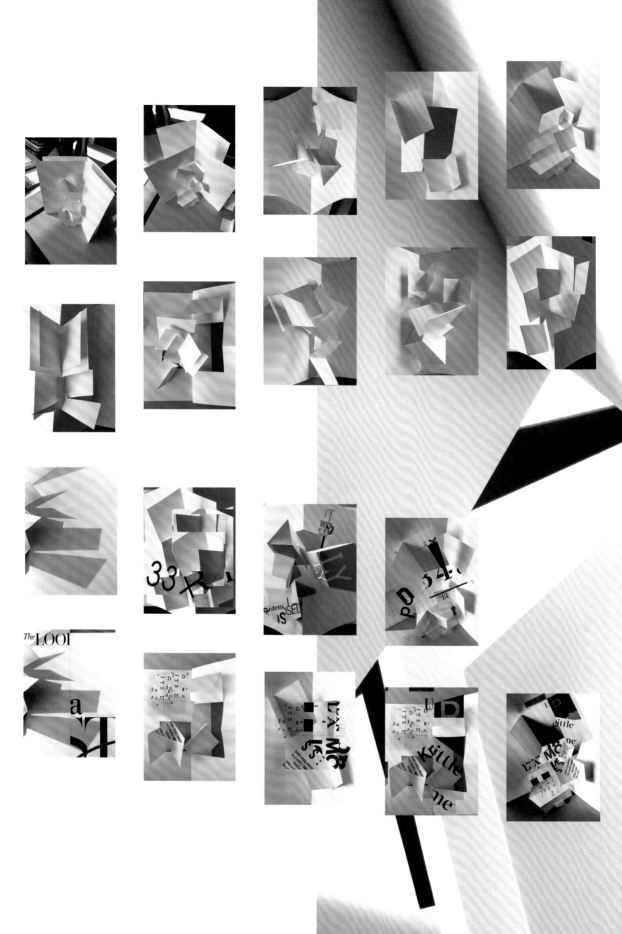

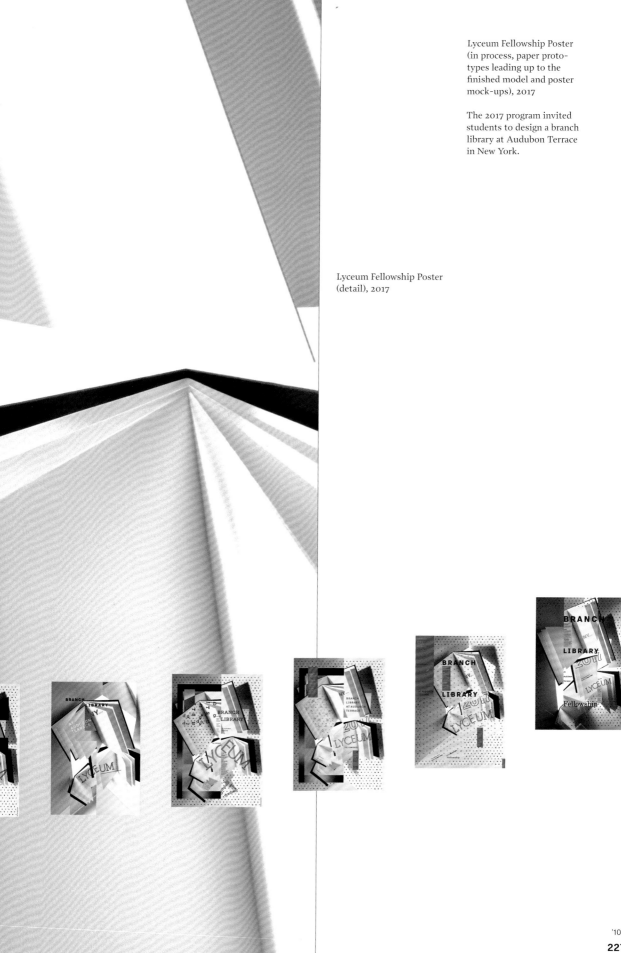

Lyceum Fellowship Poster
(in process, paper proto-
types leading up to the
finished model and poster
mock-ups), 2017

The 2017 program invited
students to design a branch
library at Audubon Terrace
in New York.

Lyceum Fellowship Poster
(detail), 2017

Lyceum Fellowship Poster
(in process, photo assembly
and type ideation), 2017.

Lyceum Fellowship Poster
(detail), 2017

Lyceum Fellowship, Student
Architecture Competition
Poster, 2017, Fuji OnSet
S-20 print, 50 ½ × 35 ½ in.

Lyceum Fellowship Poster (in process, pencil drawing and miniature paper model), 2018

The 2018 program called for students to design a community market hall and farmers' market in Guelph, Ontario.

Opposite: Lyceum Fellowship, Student Architecture Competition Poster, 2018, Fuji OnSet S-20 print, 50 ½ × 35 ½ in.

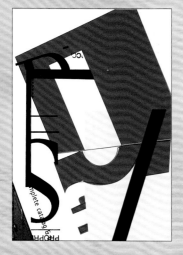
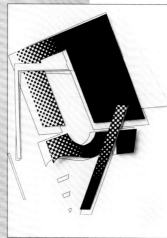

Lyceum Fellowship Poster (in process, progression from collage to sketch to three-dimensional paper prototype), 2019

The 2019 program centered on a structure to commemorate the West Coast Immigration Station, Angel Island, San Francisco.

Lyceum Fellowship, Student
Architecture Competition
Poster, 2019, Fuji OnSet
S-20 print, 50 ½ × 35 ½ in.

Reframing the Poster was an exhibition of student work from a course of the same name at Rhode Island School of Design; a wastebasket of scraps inspired the poster design.

Reframing the Poster Poster (detail, collage), 2019

Reframing the Poster Poster (process images showing evolution of collage to poster), 2019

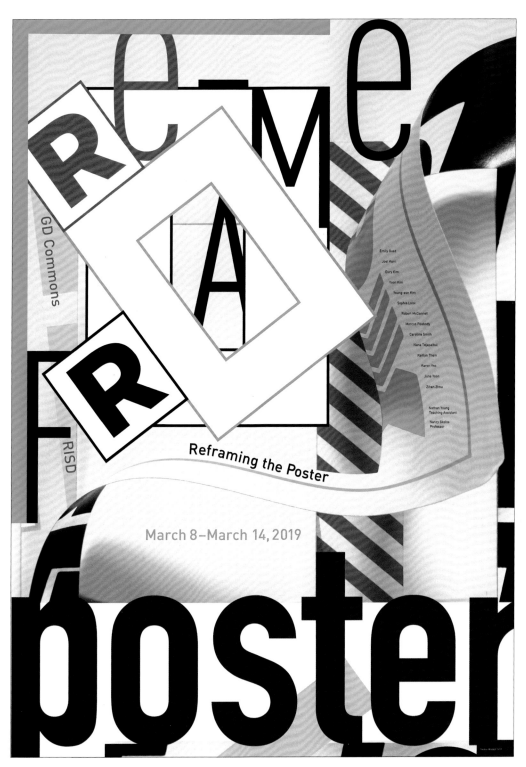

Reframing the Poster Poster,
Rhode Island School of
Design, 2019, Fuji OnSet
S-20 print, 50 ½ × 35 ½ in.

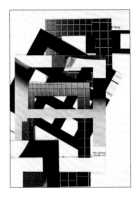

Photo set-up and exper-
iments with laser-cut
collage pieces, 2019

Photo set-up and detail
of experiments with
laser-cut collage pieces,
2019

Rich Shitting on
Poor Poster Initiative,
organized by Feliks
Buttner, 2019,
Fuji OnSet S-20 print,
50 ½ × 35 ½ in.

ter

October 14   2019

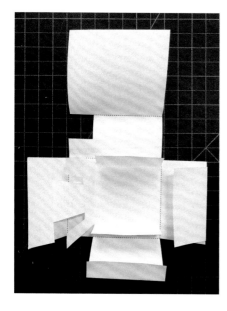

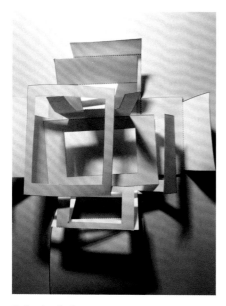

Reframing the Poster
Poster (in process,
iterations for a three-
dimensional framing
structure), 2019

Reframing the Poster
Poster (detail final
photograph), 2019

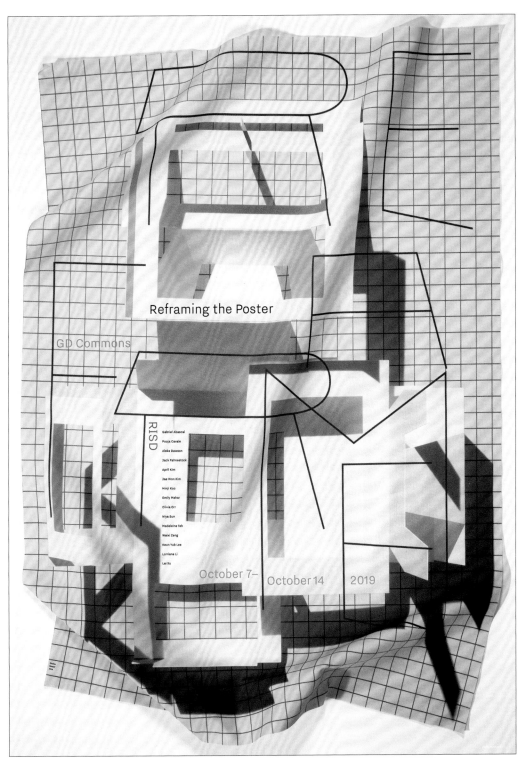

Reframing the Poster Poster, Rhode Island School of Design, 2019, Fuji OnSet S-20 print, 50 ½ × 35 ½ in.

The poster was printed on cloth, wrinkled, and rephotographed to illustrate the poster's flexibility as a medium.

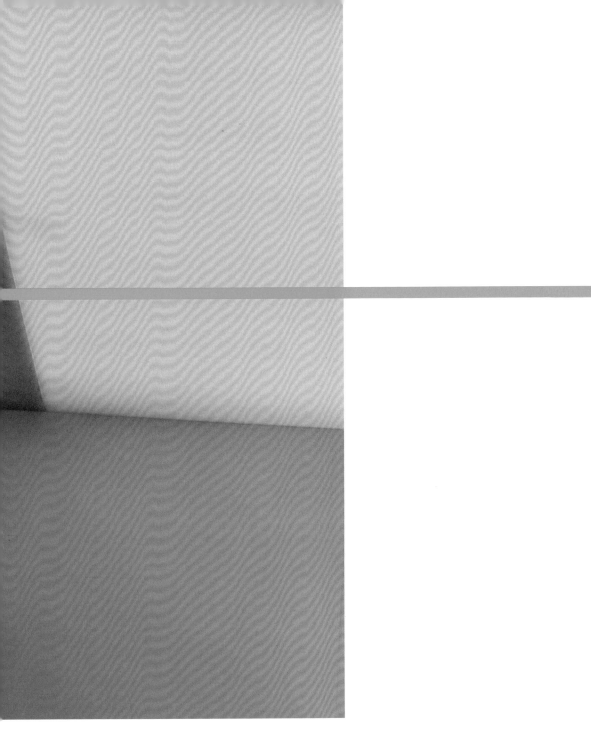

'20s: Moving Forward

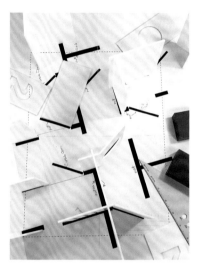

Lyceum Fellowship Poster (in process, progression of the photographic model from collage to paper mock-up to final), 2020

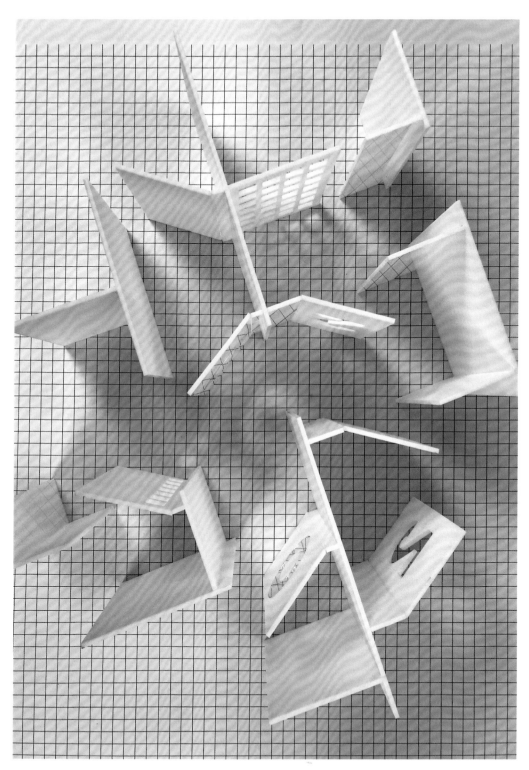

The 2020 program called
for an updated housing
prototype based on the
Chicago bungalow.

Lyceum Fellowship Poster
(in process, final model),
2020

Lyceum Fellowship Poster
(in process, preliminary
design of paper mock-up
with bungalow floorplan
superimposed), 2020

Lyceum Fellowship, Student
Architecture Competition
Poster, 2020, Fuji OnSet
S-20 print, 50 ½ × 35 ½ in.

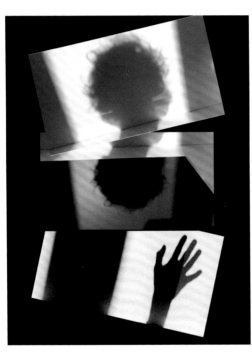

Far from Home Poster (in
process, shadow portraits
generated as frames and
assembled to create a cine-
matic personal space), 2021

Studio Collective, Annual Film
Festival, Far from Home Poster,
School of Design, Virginia Tech,
2021, Fuji OnSet S-20 print,
50 ½ × 35 ½ in.

AIGA, Get Out the Women's
Vote Poster (detail), 2021

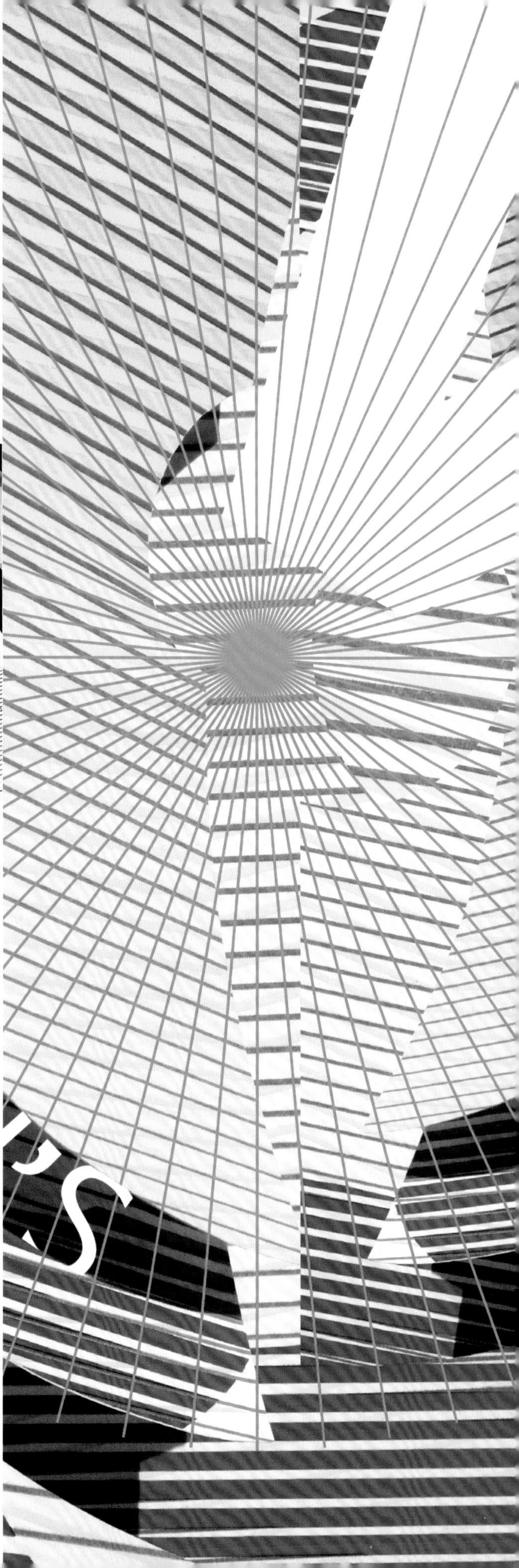

AIGA, Get Out the Women's
Vote Poster (in process, paper
prototypes), 2021

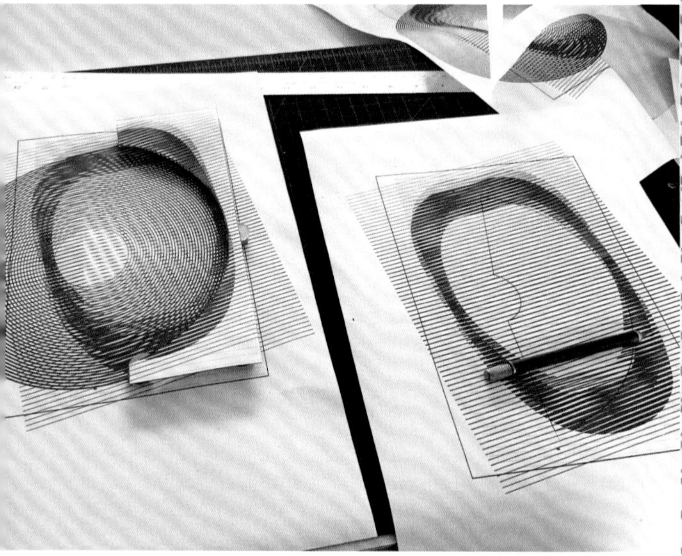

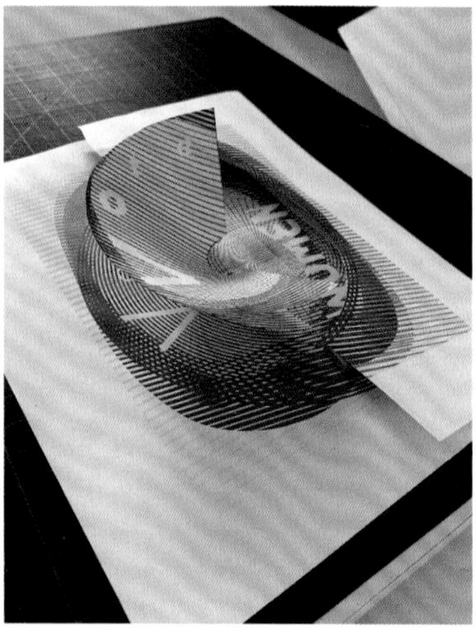

AIGA Get Out the
Women's Vote Poster,
2021, Fuji OnSet S-20
print, 50 ½ × 35 ½ in.

Lyceum Fellowship Poster
(in process, model making),
2021

Program Author:
The Theoretical Observations of Mark Ricker, FAIA

Jury:

Mark Ricker, FAIA
President, Ricker & Co
Director, Lyceum Fellowship

Molly Moore
Director of Marketing, Make Dev Space
Chair of the Lyceum Fellowship Competition Committee, Museum Museum Fellowship

Additional Jurors to be announced.

Jury

Submission Deadline: May 14, 2021

www.lyceum-fellowship.org

2021

COMPETITION

LYCEUM

A TRAVELING FELLOWSHIP

IN ARCHITECTURE

Opposite: Lyceum
Fellowship, Student
Architecture Competition
Poster, 2021, Fuji OnSet
S-20 print, 50 ½ × 35 ½ in.

The design's spade-like
shapes were inspired by
the shovel manufacturing
company of the Ames family,
whose estate in Easton,
Massachusetts, was the
competition site.

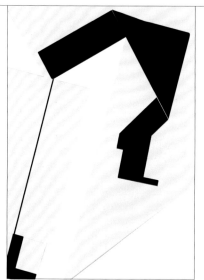

Lyceum Fellowship Poster
(in process, from collage to
final photographic model),
2021

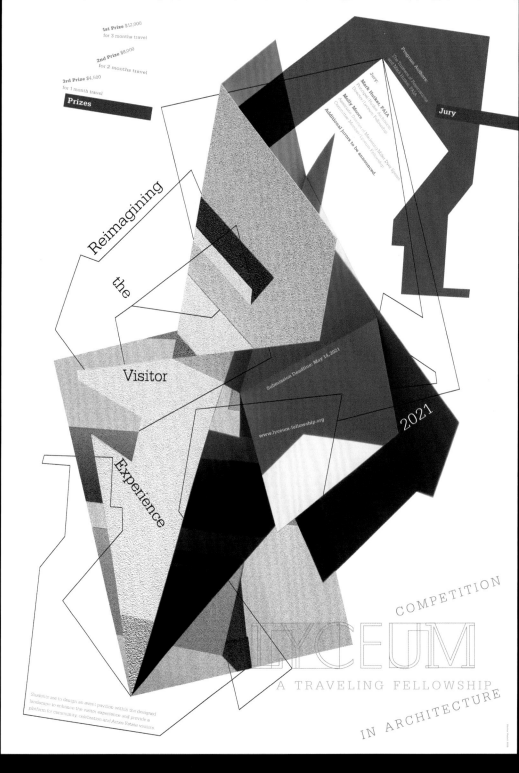

1st Prize $12,000
for 3 months travel

2nd Prize $8,000
for 2 months travel

3rd Prize $4,500
for 1 month travel

Prizes

Program Authors
The Institute of Architecture
with Maria Hurtado, FAIA

Jury

Mark Husker, FAIA
Principal Husker + Architects
Director Lyceum Fellowship

Molly Moore
Associate Professor of Architecture Mills, Dyer Smart
Operations Manager Lyceum Fellowship

Additional Jurors to be announced.

Jury

Reimagining

the

Visitor

Submission Deadline: May 14, 2021

Experience

www.lyceum-fellowship.org

2021

COMPETITION

LYCEUM

A TRAVELING FELLOWSHIP

IN ARCHITECTURE

Students are to design an event pavilion within the designed
landscape to enhance the visitor experience and provide a
platform for community celebration and Aimes Estate visitors.

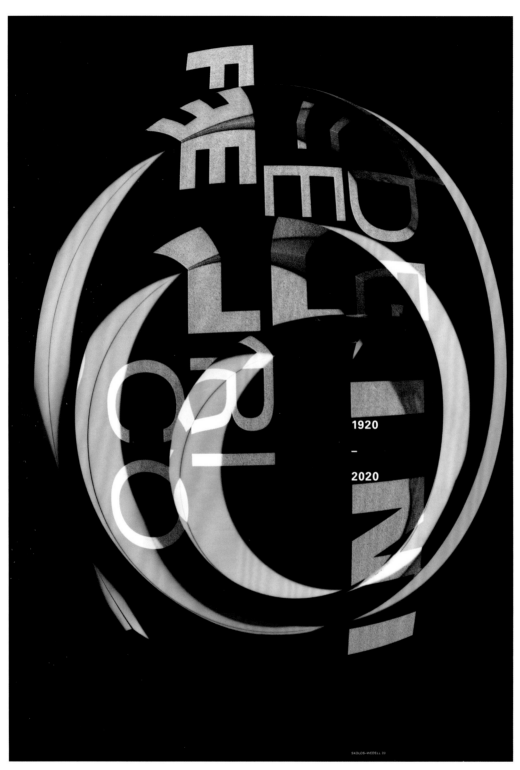

1920
–
2020

100th Birthday Tribute to
Federico Fellini Poster, 2021,
Fuji OnSet S-20 print,
50 ½ × 35 ½ in. (originally
designed for on demand inkjet
printing 39 ½ × 27 ½ in.)

100th Birthday Tribute to
Federico Fellini Poster (in
process, type layout and
final photograph), 2021

100th Birthday Tribute to Federico Fellini Poster (in process, testing the results of a set-up, placing a wound strip of reflective Mylar on top of various typographic layouts to arrive at the final design), 2021

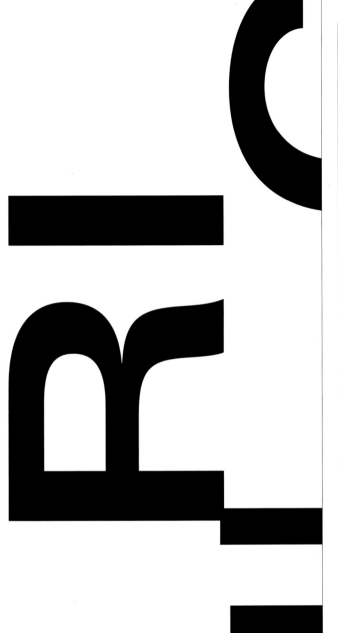

100th Birthday Tribute to Federico Fellini Poster (in process, type laser print detail), 2021

100th Birthday Tribute to Federico Fellini Poster (in process, type layout and final photograph), 2021 before it was slightly spherized in Photoshop

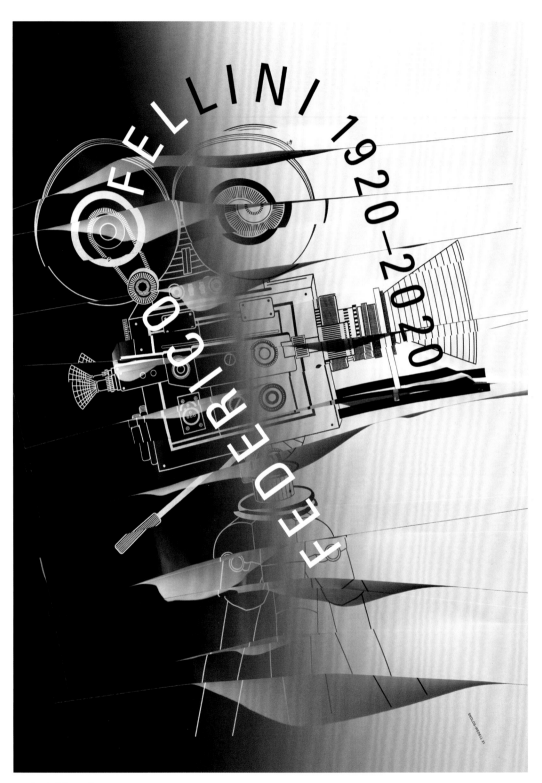

100th Birthday Tribute to
Federico Fellini Poster, 2021,
Fuji OnSet S-20 print,
50 ½ × 35 ½ in. (originally
designed for on demand inkjet
printing 39 ½ × 27 ½ in.)

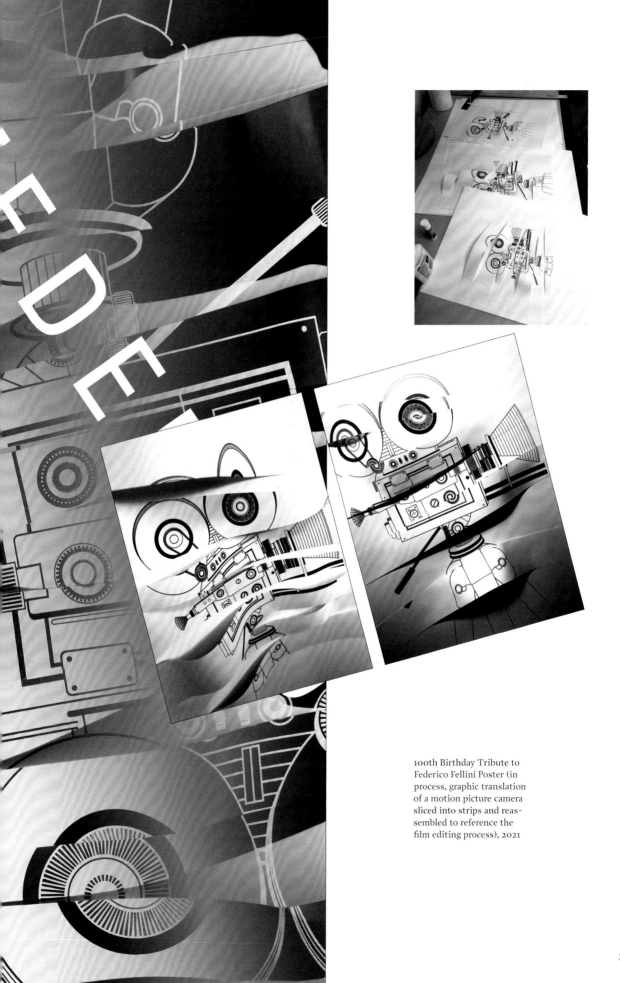

100th Birthday Tribute to
Federico Fellini Poster (in
process, graphic translation
of a motion picture camera
sliced into strips and reassembled to reference the
film editing process), 2021

Lyceum Fellowship Poster
(in process, photographic
model using tiered laser-
cut Plexiglas sheets), 2022

The design's etched graphic grids
suggest the partitioning seen at
archaeological digs and reference
the 2022 Lyceum program's
paleontological site and project
for the design of a structural
threshold leading to a historic
cave area.

Opposite: Lyceum Fellowship
Poster (detail), 2022

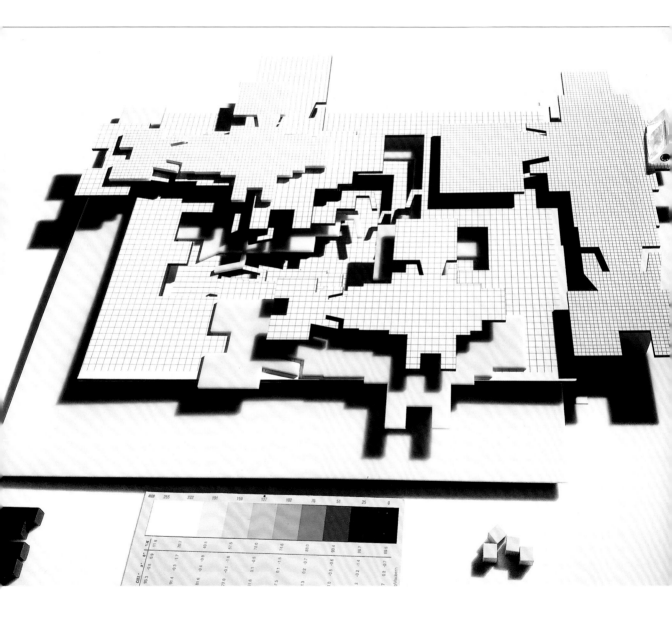

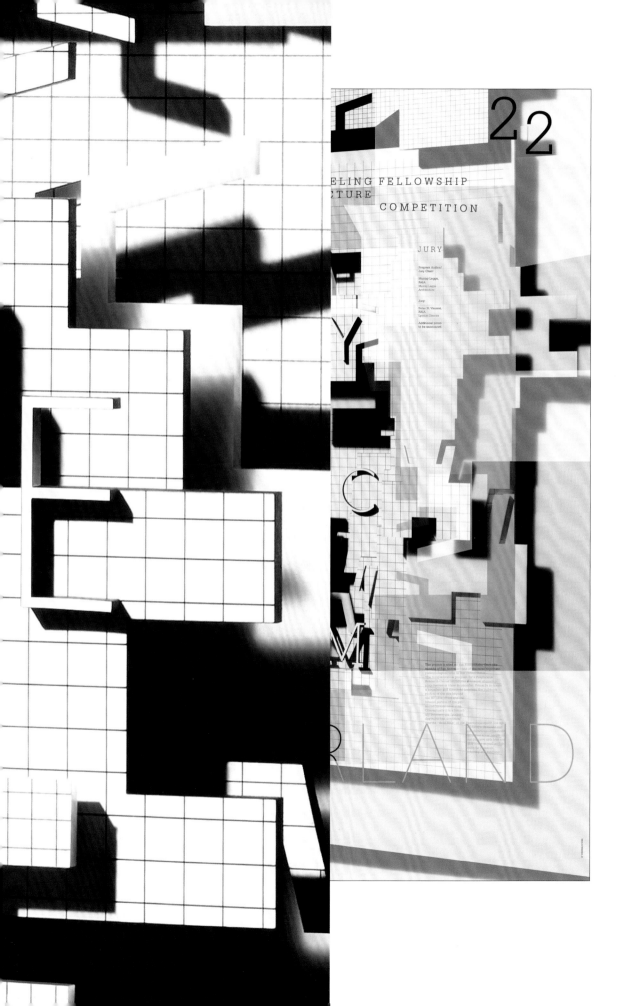

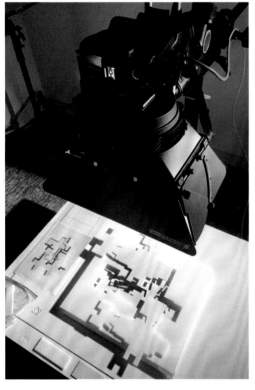

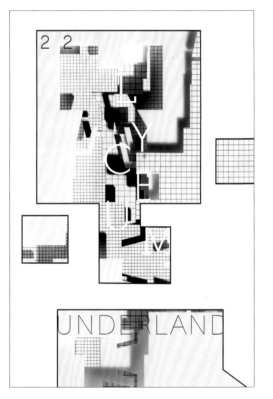

Lyceum Fellowship Poster
(in process, laser-cut
Plexiglas parts assembled
in camera), 2022

Lyceum Fellowship Poster
(in process, early poster
sketch), 2022

Opposite: Lyceum Fellowship,
Student Architecture
Competition Poster, 2022,
inkjet print, 50 ½ × 35 ½ in.

22

A TRAVELING FELLOWSHIP
IN ARCHITECTURE
COMPETITION

PRIZES

1st Prize $12,000
for 3 months travel

2nd Prize $9,000
for 2 months travel

3rd Prize $4,500
for 1 month travel

JURY

Program Author/
Jury Chair:

Murray Legge,
FAIA
Murray Legge
Architecture

Jury:

Peter B. Vincent,
FAIA
Lyceum Director

Additional jurors
to be announced

LYCEUM

Submission Deadline: May 26, 2022
www.lyceum-fellowship.org

UNDERLAND

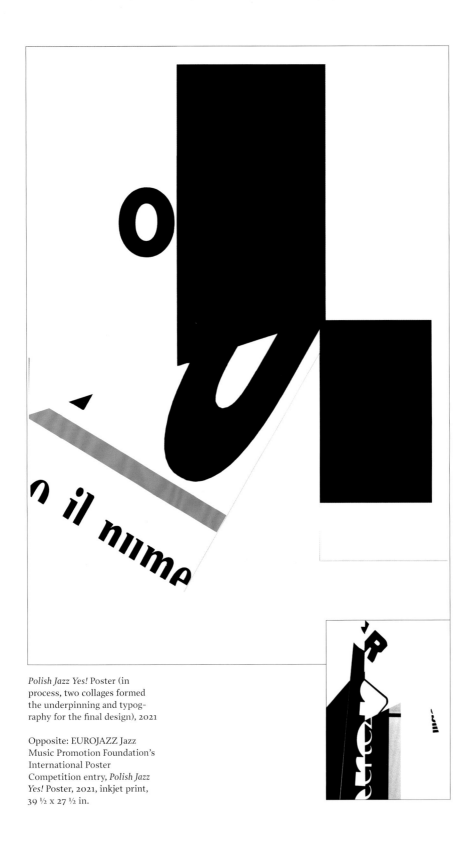

Polish Jazz Yes! Poster (in process, two collages formed the underpinning and typography for the final design), 2021

Opposite: EUROJAZZ Jazz Music Promotion Foundation's International Poster Competition entry, *Polish Jazz Yes!* Poster, 2021, inkjet print, 39 ½ x 27 ½ in.

yes!

jazz polish

radioJazz.fm

Lyceum Fellowship Poster
(detail), 2022

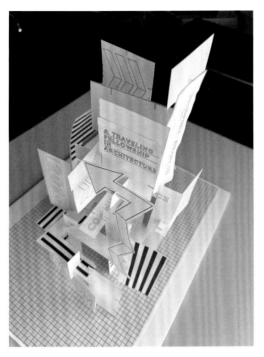

The 2023 Lyceum Fellowship design challenge was to revitalize an abandoned retail pedestrian mall in Baltimore.

Lyceum Fellowship Poster (in process, constructing a three-dimensional framework of laser-cut Plexiglas components beginning with a full scale paper model, and gluing and assembling the final structure), 2022

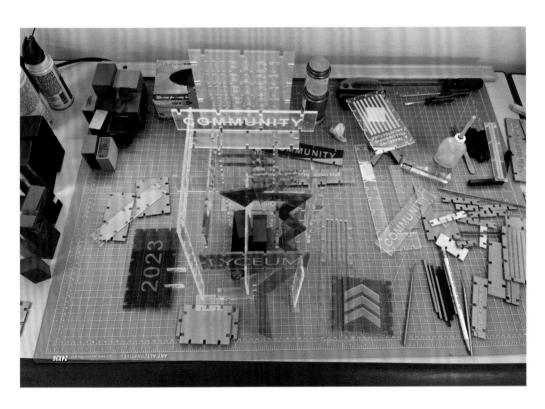

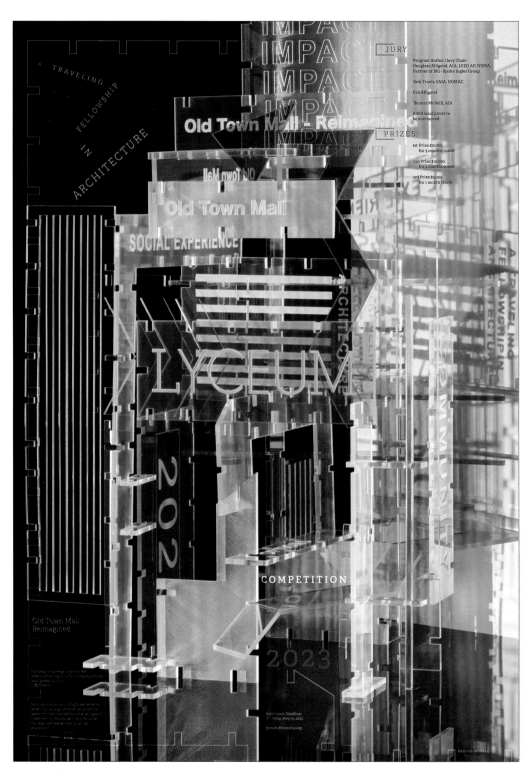

Lyceum Fellowship, Student
Architecture Competition
Poster, 2023, inkjet print,
50 ½ × 35 ½ in.

Alternate overhead camera angle. A front view was selected for the final poster image.

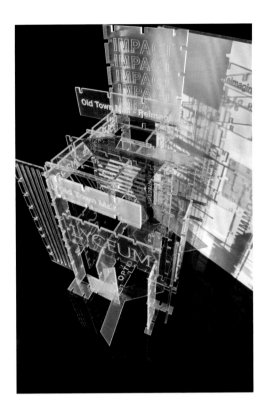

Lyceum Fellowship Poster (in process, photo shoot with overhead camera set-up), 2022

In Conversation:
Finding Magic

In Conversation: Finding Magic

N   We talk a lot about our collaborative practice, the blurring of our roles and contributions to the work. But there is a natural breakdown to some extent, which originates in our earliest training. You contribute the photographic image, the picture, and I, the text and the design, to what finally becomes the designed picture. So let's talk about the image. What are some of the key aspects of your photographic process?

T   I focus a lot on the ways in which photography intensifies our capacity to work with symbols in graphic design overall. Influences are also important—the impact of external references and individuals that have directly or indirectly affected the way we see. There's the dynamic use of light, of course. And we always keep magic in mind for all of our projects.

N   That might sound a little pretentious; people never talk about "magic." I remember when we were deciding on a title for our book *Graphic Design Process*. We proposed the title *Case Studies in Creativity* and were surprised at how strongly the publisher objected to the word "creativity," because it was too "hocus-pocus."

T   I think they felt that creativity is not measurable or quantitative. We can't say we have 30 percent magic, and we can't describe to anyone how to conjure it up, but I think we've figured out ways within our own process, like collage and chance operations, to set up situations where magic is likely to happen.

     We teach our students to have an open mind in their process. I do think you can teach people to seek magic and to understand that there is a magician working within them. For example, we might experience the sensation of "pulling a rabbit out of a hat" or juxtaposing elements that don't seem to belong, but when they are combined, they suddenly become essential content within that picture plane.

N   It's kind of surprising that you are emphasizing this aura of magic because when I watch you work and observe all the planning and industry that goes into it, it doesn't seem spontaneously magical.

T   People think of magic as "poof"—the moment the rabbit appears—but it's really all about setting the stage. When you do something quite unexpected with the image, give different points of view to the viewer, allow them to think about possibilities, or see something in an unconventional way, that's visual magic and it's emotional. People respond because they feel it. So "magic," I think, is a critical component of every piece we create.

N   Photography works so well in this regard, because it sets up a conventional expectation and then anything you do to alter it challenges peoples' perception. They aren't sure if it's real or if it's not, because they still associate photography with reality.

T   Yes, they do, although with computer-generated imagery, photography really has become something quite different. You know, it's its own medium, its own world, its own universe. However, you still equate it with reality. When you learned about photography as a child, it was the family photograph, "the snapshot," that was the direct link to experiences. The documentation of grandma and grandpa and all the kids at Thanksgiving with a camera. That was "real" because you remember it, you have at least a framework of reference to say: "When I pull that photo up, that's real, that happened." When people see one of our posters they would say, "It's real but it isn't real."

I like the idea that we can generate questions with a work rather than solve the problem and present a kind of final document saying, "Here's the absolute answer to all your questions." Instead, we're going to make you ask more questions, prompted by a particular series of symbols, images, and texts that we've combined in an unexpected way. I do think that the photograph has an advantage here—to pose questions and challenge the viewer's perception of what's going on.

N   Do you think that's a less important position to be in as a designer? A question raiser as opposed to a problem solver? I don't want to make value judgments, but we're trained in school to be strategic and solve problems, to communicate directly, so do you feel guilty that we don't do that?

T   We're operating in the middle between design and art, answers and questions, playing that middle ground where we're not going to get so subjective that people will never figure out what we're talking about or so open that any meaning could be applied. When we're working, we're looking at both sides, weighing all options in determining what that balance should be. We can't lose the essential information but at the same time, the images and the additional graphics are not necessarily crystal clear.

N   So, getting back to your way of working with photography. How did you first start taking photographs?

T   Getting into photography was a very serendipitous event. When I was young, I was a painter. Every opportunity I had, I always went out to the beach and painted landscapes and whatever else I could think of. Boats in the water, trees on the shore, all those sorts of themes, classic local situations. One day I was with a friend of mine who had a camera, and he was taking pictures of the same

to undergraduate students from invited schools who have completed five semesters of study.

thing I was painting, which was the lake shore frontage and the waves coming over the edge of a breakwater. I was trying to capture this idea of motion and the sensation of the waves. He was clicking away and while I was trying to capture the same moment, I looked at the camera and suddenly realized that for me painting is great but it's not the best way to capture time. I knew I had to get a camera immediately!

N   Who were some of your influences?

T   Once I began in photography, I think the first influences were fashion and news magazines. We had a small drugstore near our house, and it had all the magazines. The one that caught my eye was *Harper's Bazaar*, partly because of Richard Avedon's photographs. I was absolutely fascinated with how he could compose those dramatic, strong compositions in the streets of Paris and his way of photographing people. Later, I really enjoyed what he was doing with the studio portraits as well. The control he exhibited! The stark portraits, especially, but fashion shots, too, and what would happen within the picture plane. That captured my attention because it really did "talk" to me about time, a different sense of time, beyond the snapshot. It was more than just "taking a picture of grandma and grandpa at Thanksgiving." These images were about creating a moment that had magic. They made you ask, looking at a fashion model, or portrait, "What's going on here?" "What are they doing?" "What's really being said?"

As Avedon's images got more reductive, with illuminated faces against white or gray backgrounds, they became even more fascinating. Even within that starkness, all that information could be presented. That made my head spin a bit.

Hiro (Yasuhiro Wakabayashi), who was also photographing for *Harper's Bazaar*, did something completely different. He used the camera almost as a painter would. I still remember his images very clearly. They were elegant and used time in an absolutely striking way. He would "paint with light," creating images that seemed literally animated on the page. When you can animate the page and prompt more questions because it appears to be moving or appears to have moved, the image extends the moment. Avedon's images are strong, very fixed in time. They're that split-second that the shutter clicks. Hiro's images use time not as a fixed moment, but represent a multiplicity of times.

Those were the first things that fascinated me as I was introduced to photography. I thought, "Here's the camera, used two ways, used as a very exacting interpretive medium and as an expressive interpretive medium." It was a "figure out how this was done" thing initially, and then I turned to "figure out what it means."

Later, I took an interest in images that represented allegories or used abstraction. Here was another way of working—and they all appeared in the same collection of magazines. I thought that was just amazing. We didn't have the multiplicity of media that we have now, where images are so accessible. You really had to go looking, and the best place to find them was at the newsstand. Magazines made a real difference when I was starting out.

N   When you were talking about the difference between Avedon and Hiro—how Hiro used multiplicity and Avedon's vision was more fixed—you mentioned admiring Avedon's control. Say more.

T   A good example would be Avedon's *Dovima with Elephants* from 1955. Even though the subjects he was shooting, a person and animals, weren't necessarily completely controllable, his ability was to wait, to be deliberate, and to consider every second as a possible "image moment." When one elephant suddenly rises, and Dovima strikes that classical Grecian form, and her compositional relationship with the elephants becomes apparent, he shoots.

That someone could visualize that strongly—the elephant's arm or leg is in the right place, Dovima's arm makes just the same gesture. Everything is balanced, everything is flowing as if they were being manipulated by remote control. I won't say like puppets, but more like the precision of the computer. As if you could say, "You want to make that? No problem. Make that trunk come up a little bit!" Yet his image is a pure photographic image. All that perfection is right there in a photo!

Hiro's control is a little bit more serendipitous. Obviously, he thinks out the composition in advance, as we can see in the painting with light series of images he did for *Harper's Bazaar* in the 1960s. In one powerful photo, he positions his model in profile to feature an elaborate earring. The pose is strong, the face is illuminated with dramatic light, but the "spice" happens around the face where he creates a bright streak of light. Keeping the shutter open for some time, while drawing with a small point source light, he brilliantly activates the space around the subject. In addition, the camera even moves. This leaves multiple hints of the model's profile in a more transparent form, indicating where the camera may have moved several times, or the model has moved—one or the other, but you don't really know. This combination of moves makes everything come together. It's all about sequencing. You can hear the photographer asking, "How do I sequence this, which exposure first, second, third?"

N   Who were some of your influences beyond fashion photography?

T   Working with my teacher Carl Toth at Cranbrook, I couldn't escape the influence of people like László Moholy-Nagy and his use of collage, photograms, and abstractly composed photographic images. That introduced a world of symbols and meaning and a new set of questions: "What does it mean?" "Why is this next to that?" It was a whole new language, a separate language!

N   What kind of a language?

T   I think what's being developed in these compositions is a strong narrative. You're learning to read the story, a story written in images. They're worlds unto themselves that you learn to read over time, especially the collage work, which uses a multiplicity of images and links ideas through design. This is designed imagery, designed with intention, with a degree of control.

Yes, serendipity plays a part, possibly, but the primary focus is on building a complex language of images and graphics to direct us toward meaning, a world we learn to inhabit.

N   What other influences come to mind that contributed to your developing ideas of what photography could be?

T   Another strong influence was understanding the "mechanics" of photography. Being on the beach with my friend I was captivated by the camera: It's a little box, recording life! This seemed to be the perfect instrument to link all the elements of life, time, and my mounting curiosity together. I would ask, "What goes into photography? What are the elements?" Those elements, you know, are the obvious things at first: light; the way light looks on objects; how have other people used light or lighting effects; and of course, the camera itself and how it works. You're always working with the same basic elements. The big challenge was to figure out how these elements affect objects and what they do to forms. Lighting, for example: how light is applied really changes something from a boring, plain object to something very special. Large, soft box lights can create a flat sense of space, or dramatic lighting can create a deeper, more intriguing sense of space, a more dramatic way of looking at the world. It's the difference between the Doris Day films of the 1950s or '60s and film noir. The former were made for drive-in theaters, which called for extremely flat lighting. I mean, they would just illuminate everything in the sets. If you compare that to the contrast in noir films, you will see and feel the difference!

The cinematographer Gordon Willis once said, "It's just as important which lights you didn't turn on." That really made a difference in the way I thought about lighting, and what could be expressed in an image through the language of light. For me, using dramatic light, high contrast, deep shadows, as opposed to everything illuminated evenly, was unquestionably the approach I preferred to use. Gaining control of lighting was and is a real learning experience. It takes years to become skilled with it.

Digital Equipment
Corporation Capabilities
Brochure (detail final
photograph), 1992

One day I remember saying, "You know, all we're doing is blowing light around." My assistant at the time thought that was an incredible image and said, "What an interesting idea, that you can scatter light, like so much dust on a surface." It is just that: "blowing" light around to see what happens. Sometimes that's what it seems like. On occasion we have so little control over it; light is more like a powder, not a solid force at all.

N   It can be formal as well with the way you define objects using light, shaping things with light. I remember you used to just keep buying more and more lights, more spots, more specialty lights. I don't know what your record was for how many you put into one shot.

T   I did work on some large sets where I think I had sixty-five or seventy on at once. I mean, it was a lot of lights. However, they were purposeful, it wasn't just flooding the place with light. I always said to myself while working, "Light it with purpose, with conviction." Everything that needs to be shown is, with no emphasis on anything unimportant.

The Lyceum poster from 1992 (p. 96), that originated in a photograph I had constructed for a Digital Equipment brochure is a good example. Its set-up was based on the idea of a computer casing, which at the time were very plain looking. They weren't computers you hold in your hand, but austere, impenetrable containers. The idea of the photographic model was to open the casing and investigate it. I think somebody had said, "This is an open system—it's like opening up your computer and allowing things in." Those words opened my thinking, allowing me to realize, "There it is. Let's take the container and literally show it as a box opening to discover what's inside." Revealing this critical idea involved creating a collection of symbols. For example, the concept of systems architecture was represented by the facade of a classical building. The use of DEC's interpretation of a Windows operating systems, was represented by two windows inside the box.

Light was a way to represent magic, the idea of a computer as a "magic box." It has to sparkle; it has to have a sense of extraordinary power; it has to have a sense of place; and it has to have a performative quality. The whole thing has to come alive. The DEC set was also strategically designed and built to channel light through its compartments. I used a collection of small spotlights shooting everywhere throughout the model. I knew where the lights were going to go and what I wanted the effect to be in the camera, both shadows and highlights. Again, degrees of control, not complete control, because I was always looking for that moment of surprise. Even though I could anticipate from experience how the set-up would react, I wanted to be able to say, "Oh, look how that material responded." I wanted it to become alive.

N   For the Lyceum poster from 1992 (p. 96), I remember we cleared out all the computer symbols to use the "box" again because the Lyceum architects came up with a program that year involving the development of a library, which was

the perfect form to represent as a container or depository of knowledge. We redesigned the internal forms, placing maps and graphics on the surfaces, and worked with three-dimensional letterforms, allowing the headline to cascade over one edge.

T   Yes, the program's site was Columbus Circle in New York City and referenced Columbus traveling to America in 1492, five hundred years earlier; that's why we incorporated the maps.

N   We never thought it was a problem for two different meanings to be created from the same kind of setting—reusing portions of the former computer box and reinterpreting it for a new purpose. Likewise, with the Computer Technology stamp (p. 120) and the *Documenting Marcel* exhibition poster (p. 119), the cubes grew out of a concept of making three-dimensional pixels for the computer stamp, but it was so interesting, we wanted to experiment with it more, so we made a three-dimensional chess board for Duchamp. We saw so much potential in the form, we just wanted to keep playing with it. And we had so many projects going on, one would naturally feed into the next.

Can you think of another example of ours where structure and light combine to form a strong set of symbols?

T   The 2011 Lyceum poster comes to mind (p. 187). The program combined a proposed Land Art installation called *Earth Curvature*, located in the Great Salt Lake Desert, and a design for a rest area and observation pavilion. The desert site was inspirational because its dramatic spareness made it a space for focus and introspection. The proposed art piece was a row of pillars, several meters high, each separated by approximately a quarter mile. From a vantage point at the pavilion, sheltered from the harsh landscape, visitors could look out at the Salt Lake and the surrounding desert, down the line-up of pillars, and see the curvature of the earth.

As a poster image, I immediately envisioned one point perspective. Anytime you can create a single point perspective for a poster you're in great shape.

N   Compositionally it pulls you in immediately. It's got magic!

T   Photographs of the Salt Lake landscape showed small rocks covering the desert floor, with the surface becoming more crystallized as the desert merged with the Salt Lake. What struck me was the idea of what would happen if we decided to invert the physical elements of the site and make the small rocks large and the sculpture small. The idea was to exaggerate the drama of the space so the viewer might feel as if they were suddenly the size of a small desert creature looking at the world from a completely different point of view.

To create this landscape in the studio, I made a miniature version of the imagined Land Art piece with small plastic dowels and formed a variety of plaster-cast irregularly shaped rocks by pouring plaster into balloons. The client affectionately called the rocks "space potatoes." I positioned the miniature sculpture into the table-top set and used dramatic lighting to cast heavy shadows on the row of dowels and strong highlights on the rocks.

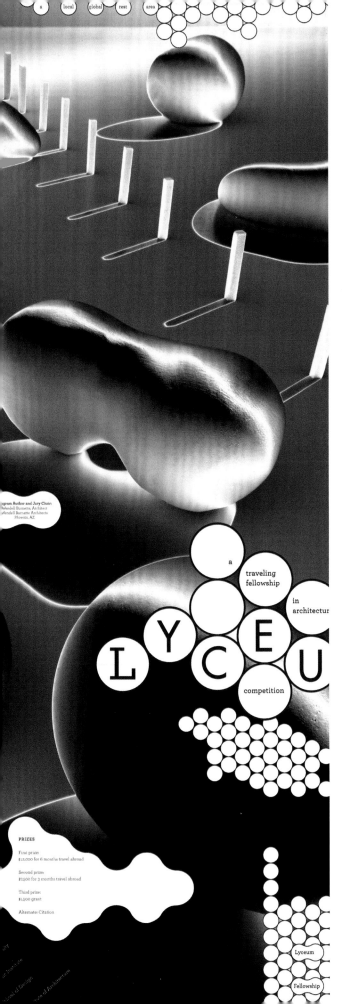

Lyceum Fellowship Poster
(details: final photograph
and final poster), 2011

Then I completed the composition by using a very wide-angle lens and forcing the perspective to exaggerate the horizon for a surreal effect. All in white—the surface was white, the rocks were white, and the sculpture was white. It looked nicely barren and captured the feeling of spareness, but at the same time it was missing something. The image didn't quite have a mood that said, "Something's going on here that's weird." I knew it needed some extra "oomph" to give it more energy.

Experimenting in Photoshop, I inverted the image, and seeing it suddenly in reverse reminded me of being in the desert at night, an experience I had in a train at dusk when it stopped briefly in the desert, and I was struck by how magical it looked. The light wasn't quite gone, but the space was just glowing. That moment when lighting isn't harsh, it isn't burning, it's simply glowing. I realized I could capture that effect through that inversion of the image. For me, that one decisive gesture created the sense of wonder I had felt while stopped that evening in the desert. Transposing it into a negative image pushed it further in the magical direction.

Your addition of the graphics added even more depth to the piece, framing the edges of the poster with illustrative crystallizations to provide a surface for the type elements, which also sat on shapes that floated through the landscape toward the date, 2011, which seemed to be setting over the horizon.

N   It's interesting, this image reminds me of some of the night shots you were doing as a graduate student at Cranbrook, in the pitch dark with strobes. What attracted you to shooting in the dark?

T   It gave me the opportunity to selectively emphasize elements of the landscape; this is lighting control again. I would position the 4 × 5 view camera on a tripod, open the lens, and walk around with a hand-held strobe illuminating the objects and areas I thought would make the most dynamic compositions. The landscape became a stage set as well, a scene with a background painting behind it. I was trying to get at this idea that when we look at a landscape, it can extend the way we see the world. The night photography was critical. It was a lighting exercise with an idea of viewer interpretation in mind.

Okay, I want to ask you about an early interest as well—your background with music as an aspiring clarinetist from a young age. Did your experience as a musician influence how you designed the Yale Symphony Orchestra posters when you were a graduate student at Yale? That was our first opportunity to really work together.

N   It was wonderful to do those posters because music was such a big interest of mine growing up, and I had to put it aside when I went to art school because there wasn't any time to fold music into the schedule. You can see in the posters, starting with the first one, the Organizational Meeting poster (p. 36), the feeling of music, with its repetition and rhythm. There's an inherent structure in music that is always in the back of my mind. Even in the Halloween Concert poster which is just a tightly cropped image of a cat positioned at the bottom of the frame with typography floating above, there is a progression of letter spacing in the title, implying a rhythm. Another example is the Firebird Suite poster (p. 39), where the wild, unpredictable structure of the feather reflects the energy of Stravinsky's music. The type was sprinkled around the edges as a kind of fringe, like the tips of the feather. I have never really analyzed how understanding music has informed my approach to design, although over the years, I've thought about it more, especially now that I've been composing music and finding that the ways I work with visual art are helping me design music.

T   Your musical background far exceeds mine, so it really helped to have your knowledge of the pieces as we were conjuring up solutions. Part of the posters' success is their emotional aspect, which I think comes from being able to extract emotions from the music and translate them into graphic representations or structures.

Your ability to tease out structure carried over into some of the initial pieces we did in the studio, where you found a framework for visual representation by looking at the engineering and construction behind various subjects.

N   The Berkeley Typographers posters (p. 48) revealed an intrinsic structure. I was looking at historical diagrams of constructed letterforms and used that formal geometry within a simple square format to express the idea of a "perfect" letterform. The Kloss Video poster (p. 62) layout is interesting too. Its grid came out of a diagram the client showed me to explain how the technology worked.

The three cathode ray tubes—red, blue, and green—reflected off mirrors onto a screen positioned a distance away. So, the poster became the room, and the tubes were in one corner and the screen was in the opposite corner. In between was a star map that came from the client's interest in Haley's Comet, which was appearing that year. He had shown me some beautiful large-format star maps, which inspired the idea of mapping the space between the projector and the screen so the video beam could stream through it like a comet.

On the heels of that was the Delphax Fonts poster (p. 75), which also involved a complex technology that we expressed photographically, in combination with superimposed graphic elements that detailed the mechanics behind the ion printer's font rendering. The floating graphic elements and dotted lines illustrated a matrix of charged ions over the o in "fonts," a cylindrical abstract depiction of the magnetized printer drum that fused the type onto the paper. These quasi-scientific structures became a fun way to represent the intricacy of the technology, not so perfectly but just expressively.

T   What do you look at first, second, third, in terms of analyzing how to address the "graphic" and "typographic" in relation to the "photographic?"

N   When combining type with an image, I think you look at the photograph first and try to figure out what its intrinsic entry points are, its rhythms, its structures, its light and dark areas—sort of the push-and-pull that's already going on with your eye in the photograph. Then you figure out if you want to reinforce those gestures with the type or if you somehow want to create more tension between them. It took us years to really develop these strategies because if you look back at our early pieces, say the first Boston Acoustics poster (p. 43), we had gotten so involved with creating the image that by the time we had to put the type on it—just two words, "Boston Acoustics"—there was barely a place for it because the image filled the entire space. We realized we needed a better approach almost right away so in our next poster for Reynolds-DeWalt Printing (p. 47) we worked the type into an asymmetrical border but were still being very timid, keeping the type and image away from each other.

Gradually we began to design the pictures with the type in mind, often being inspired by scraps of colored paper on our desks or in the flat file drawers that formed wonderful, shaped structures that began to inform the design of the photographs themselves and simultaneously develop a scaffolding for both the type and the image.

T   When we're talking about grids, we're not talking about that rigid sort of 90-degree grid that you lay out most books with, but rather more expressive kinds of grid structures that are often generated by chance. The Lyceum poster from 1990 (p. 93) is one of the first examples that shows how a found paper construction laid the entire groundwork for a piece.

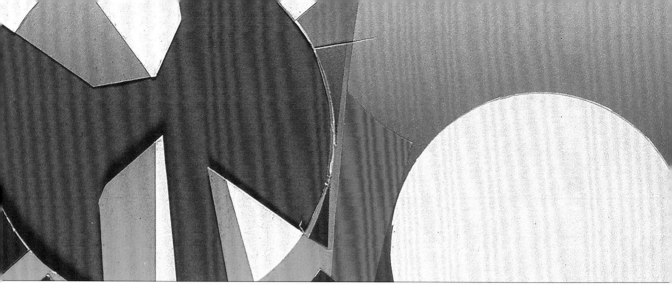

N   The great thing was that this accidental paper grid had varied sizes and shapes of modules. Some were angled and some were aligned, and it afforded a different way of thinking about the picture plane itself, which is typically so right-angled that it's hard to get past that. These unexpected structures broke open a whole new range of possibilities. I was interested in cubism, and a little later I read that Juan Gris had a very similar process, using little sketches made of paper to give him ideas for his paintings, which he called his "colored architecture." We discovered a similar strategy in our own parallel universe.

The compositions became even more interesting when we started collaging with magazine pieces, where the endless combinations of photography and text had even more potential for mixing up structure and meaning.

T   We were really looking at it as a catalyst for new kinds of graphic languages based on "collision." That became quite exciting.

N   Right? I mean, with even just a couple pieces of type, putting one in front of the other begins to overpower the other, and suddenly it creates action and meaning. And the relationship can flip if the big piece is made up of small type and the small piece is a cropped piece of large type, and you start to see all these different ways that things can relate.

The cut-up architecture magazines also began to make an even stronger connection for us between architecture and graphic design. These fragments of architectural spaces, shot with strong perspectives, pulled your eye in many directions and set up even more complex relationships. This also sharpened my perception of the dynamics within our photographs. Like the 2005 Lyceum poster (p. 155), where I literally diagrammed the photo, outlining its basic shapes to make a grid that I then flipped around to use as a framework for the typography.

I had always looked at the photo to tease out its framework but had never directly traced the shape of a photo and flipped it to make a grid. I kept using that strategy for a while. In the 2006 Lyceum (p. 161) and the 2008 Lyceum (p. 166) posters, you can also see linear elements that appear in relationship to the type.

Lyceum Fellowship Poster (in process, collage showing the origin of the structure for the shopping bag and type treatment), 2007

Opposite: Neocon 23 Poster, Merchandise Mart, Chicago (in process, sketch made from color paper scraps), 1991

T   So you translated the image into a grid so it became a grid, too?

N   Making the image into a grid, yeah, but it's also a reflected grid and often flipped to become an echo or a mirror.

T   Could you talk more about using collages to generate structures? We can look at the 2007 Lyceum poster (p. 162) as an example in which the type appeared in a collage, with a large *x* and *o* translated almost directly for their literal formal value.

N   Our idea of literal. [laughs] When starting our process for the 2007 Lyceum poster (p. 162), a collage with a giant *x* and *o* in the middle of it caught our attention because it was starting to spell "Mexico." We often combined collages, and when we placed a smaller collage into the center of this typographic one, part of its big *o* popped up behind the inset collage and suddenly created the illusion of a shopping bag with a handle on top. The idea of the poster becoming a shopping bag with type spilling out of it just sort of happened that way, and it perfectly fit the theme of the competition—the design of a marketplace in Mexico City.

That's what's so great about the collage process. It accelerates the way making art works, where you're looking at the work and it responds, and you respond back.

Another collage-inspired example was the 2001 RISD Faculty Biennial poster (p. 139), where we were looking through our collage sketches and noticed a typographic configuration that almost spelled "RISD," and another that looked kind of like a museum entrance with a colorful banner. We would just kind of daydream on the notebook pages and see things, make mental connections, and begin to generate something. Once we chose a few collages, we'd quickly scan them into the computer and start playing with them in Illustrator or Photoshop, rescaling them and combining them to see what would start to happen. Because the collage pieces contained both images and type, it automatically made it so much easier to think of words and pictures together.

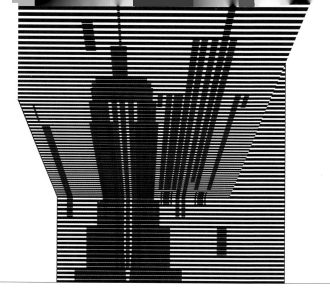

Lyceum Fellowship Poster (in process, graphic translation of the Empire State Building, printed and folded), 2015

T   Our work has almost always included such chance operations, not random thoughts but collected thoughts—focused thoughts. As we start each project, we're looking at a list of words, collages, external references, and then we sort of put them in a pot and bring them to a boil and see which ones come to the surface. So, talk a little bit about how that process has developed.

N   We have learned how to stack the deck a little bit. If we want something to happen, we figure out ways to direct it. One example might be the 2015 Lyceum poster (p. 219), where the competition problem was about the aging of the city of New York City and its people. The students were asked to take the Empire State Building and reconfigure it into a senior living center. At the time, I'd been thinking a lot about type and image and how to make letterforms sink into an image even more. In the mid-2010s we had already been working with clear Plexiglas structures to give the photographs a more ethereal presence but for this poster, we went the opposite direction. We started out by translating the Empire State Building into a black-and-white, striped image and generating multiple pieces to collage together. We applied the artwork to three-dimensional structures to create a high-contrast image, which on the surface seemed like a nightmare to put type on, but because type is intrinsically black-and-white, it automatically synchronized with the black-and-white structure. I don't think we would have ever been able to think at that level of complexity if we hadn't had the experience of mixing up random collages and seeing the payoff. We thought, "Well, if all that happens with random pieces, what if we *made* pieces?" And it's not like we calculate too much. We make a variety of elements, never exacting parts, throw them together, and see what happens.

T   With some purpose …

N   Purpose, yes. We were thinking about the energy of the city and its vibrancy and the optics of gridded window facades, but the process allowed the poster to have a life of its own.

      A lot of times it almost feels like we're molding the ideas as we're making iterations with our hands because we can't really preconceive them any other way.

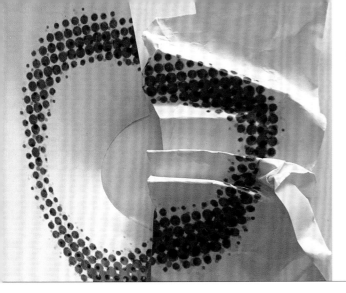

AIGA, Get Out the Women's
Vote Poster (in process,
paper prototype), 2021

The Get out the Women's Vote poster (p. 251) comes to mind. I had this idea of amplifying the women's voice and wanted to combine a mouth and a megaphone but wasn't sure how to fit them together. I quickly put together an image of an open mouth and printed out a few color laser prints, cut them out, and bent the mouths into cone shapes. I also tried crumpling some to create a contrast where the woman's voice was being discarded instead of amplified. Chance operations do happen in the computer but because of gravity or something, it just seems like things mix and fall into place differently in physical space.

T   There's a greater responsiveness in the analog method of just assembling something quickly in paper.

N   Yeah. The hand and mind work together much more quickly that way.
The computer is great but it has a kind of deliberate quality built into it that interrupts the flow because you're always having to stop and select this, and stop and select that.

T   So, when you're dealing with paper and you're molding paper and you're bending it and crunching it up to see what happens you can generate a series of models very quickly—a lot of them, and get a sense, taking pictures with the phone—of what could work and conform optically.

N   That makes me think about the time when you printed a poster on cloth, and then you threw it on the table, and it looked so cool with the irregular wrinkles that we decided we wanted the next poster we made to be wrinkled, which ended up as the *Reframing the Poster* exhibition poster (p. 241).

Another fun breakthrough was when we realized we could laser-cut magazines in any shape. We used frame-shaped elements for another *Reframing the Poster* exhibition poster (p. 235). The original idea came from a waste basket full of cutaway paper frames we generated from trimming a book comp. It was an easy process, combining line art sketches and collages that we made from bending and photographing the laser-cut frames. I also relied on typographic elements in the collages to inform the typography, substituting the placeholder words with the show title and actual information about the exhibit.

T   We were basically collaging under the camera, throwing those paper elements under the camera, and letting them do unexpected things like folding, bending, piling up, making shadows, and surprising us.

N   Another critical moment for us was writing *Type, Image, Message* in 2006 (p. 24), because we were able to articulate what we'd been doing intuitively for years. We realized the intrinsic qualities of images are so much more visceral than the elements of typographic systems, whose meanings and reading conventions are completely learned. From that point on, our mission was to figure out how to make the type more visceral and how to make the images more symbolic, so both could meet halfway. After we became more conscious of those dynamics, we had an easier time making the type and image harmonize.

For example, with the 2013 RISD Faculty Biennial poster (p. 208) we applied vinyl type directly onto spiral ribbons, so the type and image became a holistic structure. You don't usually read type in a spiral, and you also don't usually see clear Plexiglas ribbons. Analyzing the dynamics of type and image through writing that book broke open a whole new world.

T   That whole learning curve reminds me of the McCoys' description of how design approaches evolve in a sequence, from a "groping phase," where you just try everything on for size, to a "golden phase," where your discoveries from the groping phase create great work, and then finally on to a "mannered phase," where you repeat yourself and embellish so that the work gets predictable and potentially boring. That's why we're always looking for different ways to play with a structure or to challenge structural conventions.

N   Yes, and in terms of the McCoys' cycle, I'm pretty sure we've gone through it at least three or four times. Gradually we've learned to avoid the "mannered phase" through an understanding of structural integrity that keeps design elements from just piling up. Structure bolsters meaning because it is all about relationships, and relationships always have meaning.

Overlap/Dissolve Cover
(in process, positioning
the three-dimensional
letters), 2022

Tom and Nancy at *Give-
and-Take: Poster Design by
Nancy Skolos and Thomas
Wedell*, San Diego State
University, 2018

ORO Editions
Publishers of Architecture, Art, and Design
Gordon Goff: Publisher

www.oroeditions.com
info@oroeditions.com

Published by ORO Editions

Authors: Nancy Skolos and Thomas Wedell
Reflected Realities © Andrew Blauvelt
Editor: Jennifer Liese
Book Design: Skolos-Wedell
Project Manager: Jake Anderson

Typeset in *Neue Haas Unica,* designed by Toshi Omagari, 2014
and *Prensa,* designed by Cyrus Highsmith, 1999

10 9 8 7 6 5 4 3 2 1 First Edition

ISBN: 978-1-957183-31-2

Color Separations and Printing: ORO Group Inc.
Printed in China
ORO Editions

ORO Editions makes a continuous effort to minimize the
overall carbon footprint of its publications. As part of this
goal, ORO, in association with Global ReLeaf, arranges to
plant trees to replace those used in the manufacturing
of the paper produced for its books. Global ReLeaf is an
international campaign run by American Forests, one of
the world's oldest nonprofit conservation organizations.
Global ReLeaf is American Forests' education and action
program that helps individuals, organizations, agencies, and
corporations improve the local and global environment by
planting and caring for trees.